FINISH LINE

Mathematics

for the Common Core State Standards

Continental

ISBN 978-0-8454-6762-6

Table of Contents

Welcome to Finish Line Mathematics for the Common Core State Standards

About This Book

Finish Line Mathematics for the Common Core State Standards will help you prepare for math tests. Each year in math class, you learn new skills and ideas. This book focuses on the math skills and ideas that are the most important for each grade. It is important to master the concepts you learn each year because mathematical ideas and skills build on each other. The things you learn this year will help you understand and master the skills you will learn next year.

This book has units of related lessons. Each lesson concentrates on one main math idea. The lesson reviews things you have learned in math class. It provides explanations and examples. Along the side of each lesson page are reminders to help you recall what you learned in earlier grades.

After the lesson come three pages of practice problems. The problems are the same kinds you find on most math tests. The first page has multiple-choice, or selected-response, problems. Each item has four answers to choose from, and you must select the best answer. At the top of the page is a sample problem with a box beneath it that explains how to find the answer. Then there are a number of problems for you to do on your own.

Constructed-response, or short-answer, items are on the next page. You must answer these items using your own words. Usually, you will need to show your work or write an explanation of your answer in these items. This type of problem helps you demonstrate that you know how to do operations and carry out procedures. They also show that you understand the skill. Again, the first item is a sample and its answer is explained. You will complete the rest of the items by yourself.

The last page has one or two extended-response problems. These items are like the short writing items, but they have more parts and are often a little harder. The first part may ask you to solve a problem and show your work. The second may ask you to explain how you found your answer or why it is correct. This item has a hint to point you in the right direction.

At the end of each unit is a review section. The problems in it cover all the different skills and ideas in the lessons of that unit. The review contains multiple-choice, constructed-response, and extended-response items.

A practice test and a glossary appear at the end of the book. The practice test gives you a chance to try out what you've learned. You will need to use all the skills you have reviewed and practiced in the book on the practice test. The glossary lists important words and terms along with their definitions to help you remember them.

The Goals of Learning Math

Math is everywhere in the world around you. You use math more than you probably realize to help you understand and make sense of that world. But what does it mean to be good at math?

To be good at math, you need to practice certain habits. And you need the right attitude.

- You make sense of problems and do not give up in solving them. You make sure you understand the problem before you try to solve it. You form a plan and then carry out that plan to find an answer. Along the way, you ask yourself if what you are doing makes sense. And if you do not figure out the answer on the first try, you try another way.

- You think about numbers using symbols. You can think about a real-life situation as numbers and operations.

- You draw conclusions about situations and support them with proof. You use what you know about numbers and operations to provide reasons for your conclusions and predictions. When you read or hear someone else's explanation, you think about it and decide if it makes sense. You ask questions that help you better understand the ideas.

- You model with mathematics. You represent real-life problems with a drawing or diagram, a graph, or an equation. You decide if your model makes sense.

- You use the right tools at the right time. You know how to use rulers, protractors, calculators, and other tools. More importantly, you know when to use them.

- You are careful and accurate in your work. You calculate correctly and label answers. You use the correct symbols and definitions. You choose exactly the right words for your explanations and descriptions.

- You look for structure in math. You see how different parts of math are related or connected. You can use an idea you already know to help you understand a new idea. You make connections between things you have already learned and new ideas.

- You look for the patterns in math. When you see the patterns, you can find shortcuts to use that still lead you to the correct answer. You are able to decide if your shortcut worked or not.

These habits help you master new mathematical ideas so that you can remember and use them. All of these habits will make math easier to understand and to do. And that will make it a great tool to use in your everyday life!

Ratios and Percents

The ratio $\frac{10}{7}$ is read as "ten to seven."

Remember that the order each number is written in a ratio is important.

The ratio $\frac{12}{8}$ is **not** the same as the ratio $\frac{8}{12}$.

A ratio can compare single quantities. A ratio can also compare multiple quantities by adding together single quantities.

You can compare different **quantities,** or numbers, using **ratios.**

This table shows the results of an election. What is the ratio of the number of votes Ted received to the number of votes Amy received?

Person	Number of Votes
Ted	40
Gene	35
Amy	55

Ted received 40 votes. Amy received 55. The ratio of Ted's votes to Amy's votes is $\frac{40}{55}$.

Ratios can be written as a fraction, with the word *to,* or with a colon (:).

What is the ratio of Gene's votes to the total votes?

Gene received 35 votes. The total number of votes is $40 + 35 + 55 = 130$. The ratio of votes Gene received to total votes received is

$$\frac{35}{130} \quad \text{or} \quad 35 \text{ to } 130 \quad \text{or} \quad 35:130$$

SAMPLE Deborah has 4 unread e-mails in her inbox. She has 36 e-mails altogether in her inbox. What is the ratio of unread e-mails to read e-mails in Deborah's inbox?

A $\frac{4}{36}$ B $\frac{4}{32}$ C $\frac{4}{40}$ D $\frac{36}{4}$

The correct answer is B. This question asks you to find the ratio of unread e-mails to read e-mails. You are told there are 4 unread e-mails and 36 e-mails altogether. So, the number of read e-mails must be 36 − 4 = 32. The ratio of unread e-mails to read e-mails is $\frac{4}{32}$.

1 What is another way to write the ratio 13 to 6?

A $\frac{6}{13}$ C 13:6

B 6 to 13   D 13 ratio 6

2 Pete has 3 sports magazines and 5 computer magazines. Which of the following is **not** a correct way to write the ratio of sports magazines to computer magazines?

A 3:5   C $\frac{3}{5}$

B 3 to 5   D $\frac{5}{3}$

3 A theater has 150 lower level seats and 100 upper level seats. What is the ratio of lower level seats to upper level seats in the theater?

A 100:150   C 100:250

B 150:100   D 150:250

4 Yesterday, Franco rode his bike for 20 minutes and rode his skateboard for 10 minutes. What is the ratio of the time Franco rode his skateboard to the time he rode his bike?

A $\frac{10}{20}$ C $\frac{1}{20}$

B $\frac{20}{10}$ D $\frac{20}{1}$

5 Cathy has 4 dolls. What is the ratio of the number of feet on all her dolls to the number of heads on all her dolls?

A 1 to 2   C 4 to 8

B 2 to 4   D 8 to 4

6 A pizza has 12 slices. Tony ate 3 of these slices and left the rest. What is the ratio of total slices in the pizza to the number of slices left after Tony ate his share?

A $\frac{3}{12}$ C $\frac{9}{3}$

B $\frac{12}{3}$ D $\frac{12}{9}$

SAMPLE Last month, Megan and Sasha both volunteered 8 hours cleaning up their town park. What is the ratio of time Megan volunteered to the time both she and Sasha volunteered?

Answer _____

✓ The ratio of time Megan volunteered is given, 8 hours. To find the total time she and Sasha volunteered, add their times together. Since they both volunteered 8 hours, their total time is 8 + 8 = 16 hours. So, the ratio of time Megan volunteered to the time they both volunteered is 8 to 16, or 8:16, or $\frac{8}{16}$.

7 Kevin has 2 types of saltwater fish and 5 types of freshwater fish. What is the ratio of freshwater fish to saltwater fish? Write your answer as a fraction.

Answer _____

8 Denise has 6 country albums, 4 rock albums, and 2 classical albums on her music player. What is the ratio of rock and classical albums to country albums? Write your answer using a colon (:).

Answer _____

9 Karita planted 15 vegetable plants. Of these, 4 were tomato plants, 6 were pepper plants, and the rest were cucumber plants. What is the ratio of total plants Karita planted to cucumber plants? Write your answer three different ways.

Answer _____

10 This table shows the number of protons, neutrons, and electrons in some chemical elements.

Element	Protons	Neutrons	Electrons
Gold	79	118	79
Silver	47	61	47
Iron	26	30	26

Part A What is the ratio of protons and electrons in gold to total protons in gold, silver, and iron?

Answer _____

What operation can you use to help find the total protons in all three of these elements?

Part B Is the ratio of protons to electrons the same or different for each of these elements? Explain how you know.

_____

_____

_____

Equivalent Ratios

6.RP.3.a

When each part of a ratio cannot be divided by a number other than 1, it is in lowest terms.

You can reduce a ratio to lowest terms in one step by dividing each part of the ratio by its greatest common factor (GCF).

Equivalent ratios are two or more ratios that compare the same quantities. They have the same value. To form equivalent ratios, multiply or divide each part of the ratio by the same number.

Which of these ratios are equivalent?

$$\frac{10}{20} \qquad \frac{2}{3} \qquad \frac{12}{18} \qquad \frac{15}{20}$$

Write each ratio in **lowest terms.** Then compare.

$$\frac{10}{20} = \frac{10 \div 10}{20 \div 10} = \frac{1}{2} \qquad \frac{2}{3} \text{ is in lowest terms.}$$

$$\frac{12}{18} = \frac{12 \div 6}{18 \div 6} = \frac{2}{3} \qquad \frac{15}{20} = \frac{15 \div 5}{20 \div 5} = \frac{3}{4}$$

$\frac{2}{3}$ and $\frac{12}{18}$ are equivalent since both have a value of $\frac{2}{3}$.

Tables can help to compare and find equivalent ratios.

Martin measured different squares and made this ratio table.

Side Length (cm)	Perimeter (cm)
10	40
12	48
?	60

What is the missing side length from the table?

The ratios of the numbers in the first two rows of the table are

$$\frac{10}{40} = \frac{1}{4} \qquad \frac{12}{48} = \frac{1}{4}$$

For each, the ratio of side length to perimeter is 1 to 4. Divide the perimeter by 4 to find the missing side length.

$$60 \text{ cm} \div 4 = 15 \text{ cm}$$

To find a missing perimeter given the side length, multiply by 4.

The missing side length is 15 cm.

SAMPLE The ratio of Tyler's shares of stock X to stock Y is $\frac{45}{18}$. Max has the same ratio of shares of stock X to stock Y as Tyler. Which of the following ratios could show the shares of stock X and stock Y that Max has?

A $\frac{5}{3}$ B $\frac{8}{5}$ C $\frac{10}{4}$ D $\frac{15}{8}$

The correct answer is C. Tyler and Max have the same ratio of shares. First reduce Tyler's ratio to lowest terms: $\frac{45}{18} = \frac{45 \div 9}{18 \div 9} = \frac{5}{2}$. Then reduce each of the possible ratios in the answer choices to see which is also equivalent to $\frac{5}{2}$. Choices A, B, and D are already in lowest terms. Choice C reduces to $\frac{10 \div 2}{4 \div 2} = \frac{5}{2}$.

1 Which ratio is equivalent to $\frac{3}{6}$?

A $\frac{5}{10}$ C $\frac{9}{12}$

B $\frac{6}{3}$ D $\frac{10}{16}$

2 What is the ratio $\frac{24}{16}$ written in lowest terms?

A $\frac{3}{1}$ C $\frac{8}{5}$

B $\frac{3}{2}$ D $\frac{12}{8}$

3 What is the missing number in this table?

2	4	6	8
14	28	?	56

A 36   C 42

B 40   D 48

4 Keiko's computer can copy 32 files in 6 seconds. Which fraction shows how fast Keiko's computer copies, in lowest terms?

A $\frac{4}{1}$ C $\frac{8}{3}$

B $\frac{4}{3}$ D $\frac{16}{3}$

5 Rob pays the same dollar amounts each month for his rent and for his television service. The ratio of one month's rent to one month's television service is $\frac{800}{40}$. What is the ratio for six months of rent to six months of television service?

A $\frac{480}{24}$ C $\frac{4,800}{240}$

B $\frac{1,400}{100}$ D $\frac{14,000}{1,000}$

SAMPLE Jupiter takes about 12 Earth years to revolve around the sun. Uranus takes about 84 Earth years to revolve around the sun. Write two equivalent ratios comparing the time it takes Jupiter to revolve around the sun to the time it takes Uranus to revolve around the sun. Make one ratio lower terms and the other higher terms.

Answer _____

The ratio of the time Jupiter takes to the time Uranus takes is $\frac{12}{84}$. One equivalent ratio can be found by dividing each part of this ratio by 2. Another equivalent ratio can be found by multiplying each part of this ratio by 2. These equivalent ratios are $\frac{12 \div 2}{84 \div 2} = \frac{6}{42}$ and $\frac{12 \times 2}{84 \times 2} = \frac{24}{168}$.

6 The ratio of pages in Luisa's math textbook to the pages in her history textbook is $\frac{640}{800}$. What is this ratio written in lowest terms?

Answer _____

7 The area covered by the Arctic Ocean is approximately 14 million square kilometers. The area covered by the Atlantic Ocean is approximately 77 million square kilometers. What is the ratio of the approximate areas covered by the Arctic Ocean and the Atlantic Ocean written in lowest terms?

Answer _____

14 **UNIT 1** ░░
Ratios and Percents

8 This table compares the exchange rates for two different currencies on a given day.

US dollars	3	5	7	9
Euros	2.40	4.00	5.60	?

Part A What is the ratio of one US dollar to one Euro?

Answer _____

Find the equivalent ratio in lowest terms for the given pairs of numbers in the table.

Part B Todd exchanged 9 US dollars for Euros. What is the value of the Euros he received? Explain how you know.

_____

_____

_____

9 The ratio of hours Tess worked on Saturday to the hours she worked on Sunday is $\frac{6}{4}$.

Part A What is this ratio written in lowest terms?

Answer _____

Part B Is $\frac{24}{20}$ an equivalent ratio to the hours Tess worked on Saturday and Sunday? Explain how you know.

_____

_____

_____

Rates

6.RP.2, 6.RP.3.b

Some examples of different units of measure are dollars, ounces, liters, miles, centimeters, hours, and years.

The denominator for any unit rate is always 1.

Be sure to write the numbers in the correct part of the ratio associated with each rate or unit rate.

$5 for 2 dozen

$$\frac{\text{dollars}}{\text{dozen}} = \frac{5}{2}$$

$$\frac{\text{dollars}}{\text{dozen}} \neq \frac{2}{5}$$

A **rate** is a comparison between two quantities with different units of measure. A **unit rate** is a rate that compares a quantity to one unit.

To find the unit rate for a given rate, divide the **denominator** into the **numerator.** A ratio, or rate, can sometimes be reduced to lowest terms to find the unit rate. If the ratio has a denominator of 1, it is the unit rate.

Gina types 200 words in 5 minutes. What is her typing rate?

Write a ratio to compare words to minutes: $\frac{\text{words}}{\text{minutes}} = \frac{200}{5}$

Reduce this ratio to lowest terms to get the rate: $\frac{200}{5} = \frac{40}{1}$

Gina's typing rate is 40 words per minute.

Unit rates can be used to solve problems.

Stan drove 90 miles in 1.5 hours. At this rate, how long would it take him to drive 180 miles?

First find the rate Stan drives the 90 miles.

$$\frac{\text{miles}}{\text{hours}} = \frac{90}{1.5} = \frac{60}{1} \text{ or 60 miles per hour}$$

Use this rate to find the time it takes to drive 180 miles.

180 miles is 2 times greater than 90 miles, so the time it takes to drive 180 miles is 2 times greater than the time it takes to drive 90 miles.

$$1.5 \text{ hours} \times 2 = 3 \text{ hours}$$

It will take 3 hours to drive 180 miles at this rate.

SAMPLE Olivia gets paid $32 to work 4 hours. At this rate, how much does she get paid to work 10 hours?

A $64   **B** $80   **C** $100   **D** $320

The correct answer is B. First find the unit rate. This shows how much Olivia earns for 1 hour of work. The unit rate = $\frac{dollars}{hour} = \frac{32}{4} = \frac{8}{1}$, or $8 per 1 hour of work. Then multiply the unit rate by the total number of hours to find the total pay: $8 per hour × 10 hours = $80.

1 An 8-foot board of wood sells for $3.60. How is this written as a rate?

A $\frac{feet}{dollars} = \frac{3.60}{8}$

B $\frac{feet}{dollars} = \frac{3.60 \times 8}{1}$

C $\frac{dollars}{feet} = \frac{3.60}{8}$

D $\frac{dollars}{feet} = \frac{3.60 \times 8}{1}$

2 For every $50 Chu earns, he puts $10 into his savings. Which statement is true?

A $\frac{1}{5}$ of every dollar Chu earns is put in savings.

B $\frac{5}{1}$ of every dollar Chu earns is put in savings.

C $\frac{50}{1}$ of every dollar Chu earns is put in savings.

D $\frac{50}{10}$ of every dollar Chu earns is put in savings.

3 Jordyn rode her bike 10 miles in 2 hours. What unit rate describes her speed in miles per hour?

A 5 miles per hour

B 8 miles per hour

C 12 miles per hour

D 20 miles per hour

4 A bakery makes $8 for every 5 loaves of bread sold. The bakery makes the same dollar amount for each loaf of bread. At this rate, what dollar amount would the bakery make by selling 30 loaves of bread?

A $35   **C** $48

B $43   **D** $70

5 A baseball pitcher can throw a ball 120 feet per second. At this rate, how long would it take the ball to travel 300 feet?

A 2 seconds   **C** 3 seconds

B 2.5 seconds   **D** 3.5 seconds

SAMPLE A photographer charges $12 for a set of 20 pictures. Each picture costs the same amount. At this rate, how many pictures cost $30?

Answer _____

✓ First find the unit rate, in dollars per picture, charged by the photographer: $\frac{dollars}{picture} = \frac{12}{20} = 0.6$ or $0.60 per picture. To find the number of pictures that would cost $30, divide this amount by the unit rate: $30 ÷ $0.60 = 50. So, 50 pictures would cost $30.

6 One serving of vegetables has 60 calories. Write the unit rate as a ratio. Then write an equivalent ratio.

Answer _____

7 A printer outputs 75 pages in 5 minutes. How many pages does the printer output in 1 minute?

Answer _____

8 When resting, Tara's heart beats 68 times a minute. Explain why this is an example of a unit rate.

_____

_____

9 Nina jumps 225 times in 3 minutes. At this rate, how many times can she jump in 5 minutes?

Answer _____

10 An 18-ounce box of wheat cereal costs $3.60. A 12-ounce box of oat cereal costs $3.00.

Part A What is the unit rate, in cost per ounce, for the wheat cereal?

Would the cereal that has a smaller or larger cost per ounce be a better buy?

Answer _____

Part B Which is a better buy, the wheat cereal or the oat cereal? Explain how you know.

_____

_____

_____

11 This table shows the distances and times Jon walked in two days.

Day	Distance (miles)	Time (hours)
Friday	0.75	0.5
Saturday	0.5	0.4

Part A On which of these days did Jon walk at a faster rate?

Answer _____

Part B If Jon walks at the faster rate both days and for the same amount of time, what total distance would he travel? Show your work or explain how you know.

_____

_____

_____

Measurement Conversions

6.RP.3.d

The original unit is in the denominator of the conversion factor so that the conversion factor cancels the original unit.

$$6 \text{ kg} \times \frac{1,000 \text{ g}}{1 \text{ kg}} = 6,000 \text{ g}$$

Some common conversions are

1 yd = 3 ft
1 mi = 5,280 ft
1 mi = 1,760 yd
1 c = 8 oz
1 pt = 2 c
1 qt = 2 pt
1 gal = 4 qt

Each conversion factor used in a problem must include the desired unit in the answer.

To convert 10 miles per hour to feet per minute, use these conversion factors:

$$\frac{10 \text{ mi}}{1 \text{ hr}} \times \frac{5,280 \text{ ft}}{1 \text{ mi}} \times \frac{1 \text{ hr}}{60 \text{ min}}$$

The original units, miles and hours, are canceled. The desired units, feet and minutes, are part of the answer.

A **conversion factor** is a ratio of equal measure used to **convert,** or change, a rate with one set of measurements to another.

What ratio can be used to convert meters to centimeters?

100 centimeters = 1 meter, so the ratio is $\frac{100 \text{ centimeters}}{1 \text{ meter}}$.

What ratio can be used to convert pints to quarts?

1 quart = 2 pints, so the ratio is $\frac{1 \text{ quart}}{2 \text{ pints}}$.

Multiply to convert using a conversion factor. When more than one conversion factor is needed, multiply by both factors.

The speed of light is approximately 300,000,000 meters per second. What is the speed of light in kilometers per minute?

Convert meters to kilometers: 1,000 meters = 1 kilometer

Convert seconds to minutes: 60 seconds = 1 minute

Write the conversion factors: $\frac{1,000 \text{ meters}}{1 \text{ kilometer}}$ and $\frac{60 \text{ seconds}}{1 \text{ minute}}$

Since kilometers need to be in the answer, rewrite the conversion factor with meters in the denominator: $\frac{1 \text{ kilometer}}{1,000 \text{ meters}}$

Multiply the given ratio by both conversion factors. Cancel any units possible.

$$\frac{300,000,000 \text{ meters}}{1 \text{ second}} \times \frac{1 \text{ kilometer}}{1,000 \text{ meters}} \times \frac{60 \text{ seconds}}{1 \text{ minute}} =$$
18,000,000 kilometers per minute

The speed of light is 18,000,000 kilometers per minute.

SAMPLE A car travels 90 miles in 2 hours. How many feet per minute is this?

A 66 **B** 180 **C** 3,960 **D** 7,920

The correct answer is C. First find the conversion factors to convert miles to feet and hours to minutes: $\dfrac{5,280 \text{ feet}}{1 \text{ mile}}$ and $\dfrac{1 \text{ hour}}{60 \text{ minutes}}$. Be sure to set up the conversion factors so that the original units, miles and hours, will be canceled. Then multiply these factors by the rate $\dfrac{90 \text{ miles}}{2 \text{ hours}}$ to find the rate in feet per minute. Cancel like units: $\dfrac{90 \text{ mi}}{2 \text{ hr}} \times \dfrac{5,280 \text{ ft}}{1 \text{ mi}} \times \dfrac{1 \text{ hr}}{60 \text{ min}} = 3,960$ feet per minute.

1 What conversion factor would be used to convert gallons to quarts?

A $\dfrac{1 \text{ gallon}}{2 \text{ quarts}}$ **C** $\dfrac{2 \text{ quarts}}{1 \text{ gallon}}$

B $\dfrac{1 \text{ gallon}}{4 \text{ quarts}}$ **D** $\dfrac{4 \text{ quarts}}{1 \text{ gallon}}$

2 What conversion factors would be used to convert grams per day to kilograms per week?

A $\dfrac{1 \text{ gram}}{1,000 \text{ kilograms}}$ and $\dfrac{1 \text{ day}}{7 \text{ weeks}}$

B $\dfrac{1,000 \text{ grams}}{1 \text{ kilogram}}$ and $\dfrac{1 \text{ week}}{7 \text{ days}}$

C $\dfrac{1 \text{ kilogram}}{1,000 \text{ grams}}$ and $\dfrac{7 \text{ days}}{1 \text{ week}}$

D $\dfrac{1,000 \text{ kilograms}}{1 \text{ gram}}$ and $\dfrac{7 \text{ weeks}}{1 \text{ day}}$

3 A vitamin tablet contains 120 milligrams of vitamin C. How many grams of vitamin C is this?

A 0.0120 **C** 12,000

B 0.120 **D** 120,000

4 A car travels 294 miles on a full tank of gas. The car's gas tank holds 14 gallons. How many yards per gallon can this car travel?

A 21 **C** 24,640

B 63 **D** 36,960

5 Gavin drank nine 8-ounce glasses of water today. How many quarts of water did he drink?

A 2.25 **C** 4.5

B 4 **D** 9

SAMPLE A fish tank at an aquarium holds 216,000 gallons of water. The tank is filled at a rate of 1 gallon per second. How many days will it take to fill this tank?

Answer _____

First find the conversion factors to convert seconds to days: $\frac{1 \text{ hour}}{3,600 \text{ seconds}}$ and $\frac{1 \text{ day}}{24 \text{ hours}}$. Be sure to set up the conversion factors so that the original unit, seconds, will be canceled and the desired unit, days, will be in the answer. Then multiply these factors by the number of gallons. Cancel like units.

$$216,000 \text{ gal} \times \frac{1 \text{ sec}}{1 \text{ gal}} \times \frac{1 \text{ hr}}{3,600 \text{ sec}} \times \frac{1 \text{ day}}{24 \text{ hr}} = 2.5 \text{ days}$$

6 What are the conversion factors to convert miles per hour to yards per second?

Answer _____

7 Helen earns $15 per hour at her job. She works 30 hours a week. How much money does Helen earn in one year if she works every week?

Answer _____

8 Cecile walked 5 miles in 2 hours. How many feet per second did she walk?

Answer _____

9 A 2-liter bottle of juice costs $2.50. Sam wants to know the cost per kiloliter.

Part A What is the conversion factor to change liters to kiloliters?

Answer _____

Part B What is the cost per kiloliter? Show your work or explain how you know.

_____

_____

_____

10 One knot equals one nautical mile per hour. One nautical mile equals 1,852 meters.

What are the original units to be canceled? What are the desired units for the answer?

Part A What conversion factors are used to convert knots to meters per second?

Answer _____

Part B What is the speed, in meters per second, of a ship traveling at a rate of 9 knots? Show your work or explain how you know.

_____

_____

_____

Percents

6.RP.3.c

Percent means "per 100." A percent can be written as a fraction with a denominator of 100.

$$\frac{25}{100} = 25\% \qquad \frac{8}{100} = 8\%$$

To change a percent to a decimal, move the decimal point two places to the left. Then drop the percent symbol.

$$46\% = 0.46$$
$$30\% = 0.30$$
$$2\% = 0.02$$

If a decimal point is not shown in a number, it immediately follows the last digit in the number.

$$6 = 6.0$$
$$473 = 473.0$$

To find the whole, divide.

$$whole = \frac{part}{percent}$$

To find the percent, divide. Then move the decimal point two places to the right and include the percent symbol.

$$percent = \frac{part}{whole}$$

A **percent** is a ratio that compares a number to 100. The **percent symbol**, %, is written after the number to show a percent.

The **percent equation** *whole* × *percent* = *part* is used to help solve percent problems. You can use this equation to find the part, the whole, or the percent.

In Joey's middle school, 64 students take Spanish. Of these, 25% are sixth graders. How many sixth graders take Spanish?

You are given the whole, 64, and the percent, 25%. You want to find the part.

Set up a percent equation: 64 × 25% = *part*

Change the percent to a decimal: 64 × 0.25 = *part*

Multiply: 64 × 0.25 = 16 sixth graders take Spanish

In a survey, 20 people said they own a laptop computer. This represents 40% of the total people surveyed. How many total people were surveyed?

The part is 20 and the percent is 40%. Find the whole.

Set up a percent equation: *whole* × 40% = 20

Change the percent to a decimal: *whole* × 0.40 = 20

Divide the part by the decimal: $whole = \frac{20}{0.40} = 50$ people

What percent of 24 is 18?

The whole is 24 and the part is 18. Find the percent.

Set up a percent equation: 24 × *percent* = 18

Divide the part by the whole. Change the decimal to a percent.

$$percent = \frac{18}{24} = 0.75 = 75\% \qquad 18 \text{ is } 75\% \text{ of } 24.$$

SAMPLE The total area of Earth covered by water is about 350 million square kilometers. This represents about 70% of Earth's total surface area. What is the approximate total surface area of Earth?

    A 245 million km²   **C** 420 million km²

    B 280 million km²   **D** 500 million km²

> The correct answer is D. You know the part, 350, and the percent, 70%. You want to find the whole. To do this, first change the percent to a decimal: 70% = 0.7. Then set up the percent equation to divide the part by the decimal: $whole = \frac{350}{0.7} = 500$. The total surface area is about 500 million km².

1 How is 5% written as a decimal?

    A 0.05   **C** 0.5

    B 0.005   **D** 5.0

2 What percent is equal to 0.9?

    A 0.009%   **C** 9%

    B 0.9%   **D** 90%

3 Teresa used a calculator to find 35% of 50. What number did Teresa get?

    A 15   **C** 50.35

    B 17.5   **D** 175

4 About 66% of each water molecule is made up of hydrogen. About how many hydrogen molecules are in 500 molecules of water?

    A 165   **C** 330

    B 250   **D** 434

5 A serving of beans has 3 grams of fiber. This is about 12% of the recommended daily amount of fiber. How many grams of fiber are in the recommended daily amount?

    A 9   **C** 25

    B 15   **D** 36

6 Padma wrote 3 pages of a 10-page report. What percent of the report did Padma write?

    A 3%   **C** 30%

    B 13%   **D** 33%

7 The population of Erik's school increased by 5% from last year to this year. This year, there were 15 more students in his school than last year. How many students were in Erik's school last year?

    A 75   **C** 750

    B 300   **D** 3,000

SAMPLE A coat is on sale for 20% off. The regular price of the coat is $60. What is the sale price?

Answer _____

> ✔ First find the dollar amount discounted. In the percent equation, this represents the part. You are given the whole, $60, and the percent, 20%: *part* = $60 × 20% = $60 × 0.20 = $12. The coat is discounted $12. To find the sale price, subtract the discounted amount from the regular price: $60 − $12 = $48. The sale price is $48.

8 Lyle leaves a 15% tip for a lunch bill of $12. What amount tip does Lyle leave?

Answer _____

9 Candice multiplies 75 × 0.6 to find 6% of 75. Will she get the correct answer? Explain how you know.

_____

_____

10 Manuel's total credit card bill last month was $250. Of that, he paid back $50. What percent of his credit card bill did Manuel pay?

Answer _____

11 Seth found that 75% of 60 is the same as 30% of another number, *n*. What is the value *n?*

Answer _____

Read the problem. Write your answer to each part.

12 This circle graph shows some amounts of money Cherish budgeted for her monthly expenses.

CHERISH'S MONTHLY EXPENSES

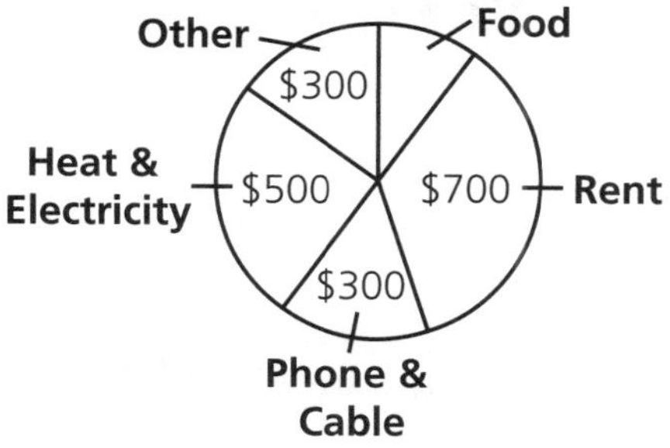

Other
$300
Food
Heat & Electricity
$500
$700
Rent
$300
Phone & Cable

Part A The amount set aside for rent represents 35% of the total money Cherish budgeted for her monthly expenses. What is the total amount of money Cherish budgeted for her monthly expenses? Show your work.

Set up the percent equation. What information from this equation are you given? What information do you need to find?

Answer ______________________

Part B What percent of her monthly expenses did Cherish set aside for food? Show your work or explain how you know.

____

____

____

REVIEW

Ratios and Percents

1 A car lot sold 9 cars and 4 trucks yesterday. What is the ratio of cars sold to trucks sold?

    A 4 : 9   **C** 4 : 13

    B 9 : 4   **D** 9 : 13

2 What is the ratio $\frac{6}{42}$ written in lowest terms?

    A $\frac{1}{4}$ **C** $\frac{1}{7}$

    B $\frac{1}{6}$ **D** $\frac{2}{7}$

3 Of the 50 players in a school band, 12% play a woodwind instrument. How many players play a woodwind instrument?

    A 6   **C** 24

    B 12   **D** 38

4 What conversion factor would be used to convert inches to yards?

    A $\frac{1 \text{ yard}}{12 \text{ inches}}$ **C** $\frac{1 \text{ yard}}{36 \text{ inches}}$

    B $\frac{12 \text{ inches}}{1 \text{ yard}}$ **D** $\frac{36 \text{ inches}}{1 \text{ yard}}$

5 Fran can address 10 envelopes in 8 minutes. What unit rate describes the number of envelopes Fran can address?

    A 1.25 envelopes per minute

    B 2.5 envelopes per minute

    C 2.5 envelopes per 2 minutes

    D 5 envelopes per 4 minutes

6 What is the ratio of tails to paws for 5 cats?

    A 1 to 5   **C** 5 to 10

    B 5 to 1   **D** 5 to 20

7 A magazine has 64 total pages and 12 full pages of ads. What is the ratio of ad pages to total pages, written in lowest terms?

    A $\frac{1}{4}$ **C** $\frac{3}{16}$

    B $\frac{1}{8}$ **D** $\frac{6}{32}$

8 Grace rode her bike 5 miles in 20 minutes. At this rate, how many miles can she ride her bike in 30 minutes?

    A 7.5   **C** 12.5

    B 9   **D** 15

9 Jason collected 80 postcards. Of these, 16 were from foreign countries. What percent were from foreign countries?

Answer _____

10 Each pair of numbers in this table form equivalent fractions. What is the missing number in this table?

Numerator	15	20	25
Denominator	24	?	40

Answer _____

11 A recipe for fruit salad calls for 2 cups of strawberries, 1 cup of blueberries, 3 cups of melon, and 2 cups of grapes. What is the ratio of total cups of fruit to cups of berries? Write your answer as a fraction.

Answer _____

12 Mr. Sanchez's driveway is 0.25 kilometer long. How many centimeters is this?

Answer _____

13 The ratio of chickens to cows on a farm is $\frac{60}{48}$. Explain whether $\frac{20}{16}$ is an equivalent ratio to $\frac{60}{48}$.

_____

_____

14 Madison paid 5% sales tax on a new backpack. The total sales tax she paid was $2. What was the price of the backpack?

Answer _____

15 A horse can gallop at a rate of 30 miles per hour.

    Part A How many yards per minute is this?

        Answer _____

    Part B At this rate, how long will it take the horse to run a race of 1,100 yards?

        Answer _____

16 Wendy works 35 hours in 5 days.

    Part A Write a unit rate to describe the number of hours Wendy works.

        Answer _____

    Part B Write an equivalent ratio for the number of hours Wendy works.

        Answer _____

17 A soup recipe calls for 6 cups of broth. A chef will triple this recipe. He wants to know how many quarts of broth he will need.

    Part A How many quarts of broth will the chef need?

        Answer _____

    Part B Explain how you solved this problem.

    _____

    _____

    _____

Dividing Whole Numbers

6.NS.2

Division is the opposite of multiplication. A **quotient** is the answer to a division problem.

> The **dividend** is the number being divided. The **divisor** is the number that divides.
>
> Divisor
> ↓
> $8\,\overline{)360}$ ← Dividend

A warehouse receives 18 boxes. Each weighs the same amount. The total weight of the boxes is 810 pounds. What is the weight of each box?

Divide 810 by 18.

```
        45  ← Quotient
  18)810
     72
     ──
      90
      90
      ──
       0
```

$810 \div 18 = 45$ Each box weighs 45 pounds.

Decimals are used when a quotient has a remainder. The decimal part of the quotient represents the value of the remainder.

Adding 0's to the right of a decimal point does not change the value of the number.

$6 = 6.0 = 6.00$

Be sure to line up the decimal point in the quotient with the decimal point in the dividend.

Some division problems divide two whole numbers that result in a **decimal quotient.** To solve these, divide the numbers and add a decimal point to the dividend and in the quotient directly above the decimal point in the dividend. Add 0's after the decimal in the dividend and bring them down to the remainder as needed until the remainder is 0.

Four friends buy bus tickets. They pay a total of $198. Each bus ticket costs the same. What is the cost of each ticket?

Divide 198 by 4.

```
       49.5     Add a decimal point to the quotient
  4)198.0       and to the dividend.
    16 ↓
    ──
    38
    36
    ──
     20    Bring down the 0.
     20
     ──
      0    Remainder is 0. Stop.
```

$198 \div 4 = 49.5$ Each ticket costs $49.50.

SAMPLE A truck travels at a rate of 60 miles per hour. At this rate, how long will it take the truck to travel 165 miles?

    A 1.65 hours   **B** 2.75 hours   **C** 3.5 hours   **D** 6.0 hours

> The correct answer is B. To find the number of hours, divide 165 by 60. Add 0's in the dividend and bring them down until the remainder is 0.
>
> It will take the truck 2.75 hours.

$$
\begin{array}{r}
2.75 \\
60\overline{)165.00} \\
\underline{120} \\
450 \\
\underline{420} \\
300 \\
\underline{300} \\
0
\end{array}
$$

1 A total of 144 children signed up for camp. They will be divided into equal groups of 16. How many children will be in each group?

    A 6   **C** 8

    B 7   **D** 9

2 Angela borrowed $1,500 from the bank. She will pay back this amount in 12 equal payments. What is the amount of each payment Angela will make?

    A $120   **C** $135

    B $125   **D** $150

3 A bookstore sold 73 copies of the same book one weekend. The total amount the bookstore received from the 73 books was $1,241. How much did the bookstore receive from each book?

    A $17   **C** $21

    B $19   **D** $23

4 A group of 28 people bought tickets to a museum. The total cost for the tickets was $315. What was the cost of each ticket?

    A $11.00   **C** $11.50

    B $11.25   **D** $11.70

5 A building is 222 feet tall and has 24 floors. The height of each floor is the same. What is the height of each floor?

    A 8.25 feet   **C** 9.25 feet

    B 8.6 feet   **D** 9.6 feet

6 An airplane reaches a maximum height of 34,320 feet. There are 5,280 feet in 1 mile. What is the maximum height, in miles, this airplane reaches?

    A 6.5 miles   **C** 7.2 miles

    B 6.8 miles   **D** 7.5 miles

SAMPLE A school bought 25 new computers. The total cost for the computers was $19,245. Each computer cost the same amount. What was the cost for each computer?

Answer _____

To find the cost of each computer, divide 19,245 by 25. Add 0's in the dividend and bring them down until the remainder is 0.

$$
\begin{array}{r}
769.8 \\
25\overline{)19,245.0} \\
175 \\
\overline{174} \\
150 \\
\overline{245} \\
225 \\
\overline{200} \\
200 \\
\overline{0}
\end{array}
$$

Each computer cost $769.80.

7 A movie theater has a total of 7 theaters. Each theater has the same number of seats. All together, the theater has 1,351 seats. How many seats are in each theater? Show your work.

Answer _____

8 What is the quotient of 148 ÷ 32? Show your work.

Answer _____

9 Shannon takes a class to learn Japanese. The class costs $243 and lasts for 12 weeks. What is the cost, per week, of the Japanese class? Show your work.

Answer _____

10 A market research company plans to survey 4,000 people about their thoughts on an upcoming election. The research company has 16 employees. Each employee will survey the same number of people.

Part A How many people will each employee survey? Show your work.

Answer _____

Part B The total amount of money each of the 16 employees earns for doing the survey is $3,400. How much money do the employees earn for each person they survey? Show your work.

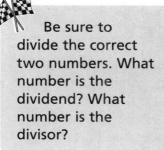

Be sure to divide the correct two numbers. What number is the dividend? What number is the divisor?

Answer _____

Dividing Fractions

6.NS.1

The product of a number and its reciprocal is always 1.

To multiply fractions, multiply the numerators. Then multiply the denominators.

$$\frac{2}{3} \times \frac{4}{5} = \frac{2 \times 4}{3 \times 5} = \frac{8}{15}$$

To change a **mixed number** to a fraction greater than 1, multiply the whole number part by the denominator. Then add the numerator. This becomes the new numerator of the fraction. The denominator stays the same.

To change a fraction greater than 1 to a mixed number, divide the numerator by the denominator. Write the remainder as a fraction.

To divide fractions, multiply by the **reciprocal** of the second fraction. The numerator and denominator of a reciprocal switch places.

What is the reciprocal of each number?

$$\frac{5}{6} \qquad \frac{1}{8} \qquad 2$$

Switch the numerator and the denominator.

The reciprocal of $\frac{5}{6}$ is $\frac{6}{5}$.

The reciprocal of $\frac{1}{8}$ is $\frac{8}{1} = 8$.

As a fraction, $2 = \frac{2}{1}$. The reciprocal of $\frac{2}{1}$ is $\frac{1}{2}$.

What is the quotient of $\frac{3}{4} \div \frac{3}{8}$?

First rewrite as multiplication using the reciprocal of $\frac{3}{8}$.

The reciprocal of $\frac{3}{8}$ is $\frac{8}{3}$, so the equivalent multiplication expression is $\frac{3}{4} \times \frac{8}{3}$.

Multiply and reduce to lowest terms if necessary.

$$\frac{3}{4} \times \frac{8}{3} = \frac{24}{12} = 2$$

The quotient of $\frac{3}{4} \div \frac{3}{8} = 2$.

SAMPLE Travis has a 6-foot long rope. He ties a knot in the rope every $\frac{2}{3}$ foot. How many knots are tied in the rope?

    A 4   **B** 8   **C** 9   **D** 12

The correct answer is C. To find the number of knots, divide 6 by $\frac{2}{3}$. First write 6 as the fraction $\frac{6}{1}$. Use it to write the division problem: $\frac{6}{1} \div \frac{2}{3}$. Multiply by the reciprocal of $\frac{2}{3}$ and reduce: $\frac{6}{1} \times \frac{3}{2} = \frac{18}{2} = 9$ knots. Choice A is not correct because the numbers are multiplied, not divided. Choices B and D are not correct because a mathematical error was made.

1 What is the reciprocal of $\frac{5}{4}$?

    A $\frac{1}{4}$ **C** $\frac{4}{5}$

    B $\frac{4}{4}$ **D** $\frac{5}{5}$

2 Which number sentence shows the product of a number and its reciprocal?

    A $\frac{2}{7} \times 0 = 0$ **C** $\frac{2}{7} \times 1 = \frac{2}{7}$

    B $\frac{2}{7} \times \frac{7}{2} = 1$ **D** $\frac{2}{7} \times \frac{2}{7} = \frac{4}{49}$

3 A hiking trail is $\frac{4}{5}$-mile long. A total of 8 markers are placed equal distances apart to help guide hikers. How far is one marker from the next?

    A $\frac{1}{10}$ mi   **C** $\frac{5}{32}$ mi

    B $\frac{2}{5}$ mi   **D** $\frac{32}{5}$ mi

4 What is the quotient of $\frac{3}{10} \div \frac{5}{12}$?

    A $\frac{1}{8}$ **C** $\frac{5}{6}$

    B $\frac{4}{11}$ **D** $\frac{18}{25}$

5 A piece of land is $\frac{2}{3}$ acre. It is divided evenly into 3 pieces. What is the size of each piece of land?

    A $\frac{1}{3}$ acre   **C** 2 acres

    B $\frac{2}{9}$ acre   **D** $2\frac{1}{3}$ acres

6 A bottle contains 8 cups of juice. The juice is poured into glasses that hold $\frac{3}{4}$ cup each. How many glasses can be filled with the juice?

    A 6   **C** $10\frac{2}{3}$

    B $8\frac{3}{4}$ **D** 12

SAMPLE Carmen walked $2\frac{1}{2}$ miles in $\frac{3}{4}$ hour. What was her average walking speed, in miles per hour?

Answer _____

> To find the average walking speed, divide $2\frac{1}{2}$ by $\frac{3}{4}$. Change the mixed number to a fraction: $2\frac{1}{2} = \frac{2 \times 2 + 1}{2} = \frac{5}{2}$. Now divide: $\frac{5}{2} \div \frac{3}{4} = \frac{5}{2} \times \frac{4}{3} = \frac{20}{6} = \frac{10}{3}$. The fraction $\frac{10}{3} = 10 \div 3 = 3\frac{1}{3}$. The average walking speed was $3\frac{1}{3}$ miles per hour.

7 It rained a total of $\frac{2}{3}$ inch in 4 hours. What was the average amount of rainfall each hour? Show your work.

Answer _____

8 A recipe makes a total of 5 cups of pudding. A serving of pudding is $\frac{3}{4}$ cup. How many servings of pudding does the recipe make? Show your work.

Answer _____

9 Horses are measured in units called hands. One hand equals $\frac{1}{3}$ foot. A horse is $5\frac{1}{3}$ feet tall. How tall is this horse in hands? Show your work.

Answer _____

10 Jada surveyed some students to see which tool they most favored for communicating with friends. The results of her survey are shown in this circle graph.

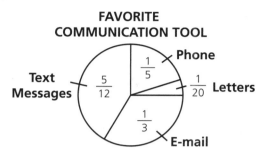

FAVORITE COMMUNICATION TOOL

Part A   What is the reciprocal of each fraction in the circle graph?

Answer _____

Part B   A total of 50 students said they favored text messages to communicate with friends. How many total students did Jada survey? Show your work or explain how you know.

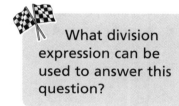

What division expression can be used to answer this question?

_____

_____

_____

Adding and Subtracting Decimals

6.NS.3

Zeros can be used as placeholders when adding or subtracting decimals.

2.050
+4.265

Adding 0's to the right of a decimal point does not change the value of the number.

2.7 = 2.70 = 2.700

You can estimate to check the reasonableness of your answers.

4.265 rounds to 4.
3.39 rounds to 3.

4
−3
1

The answer should be close to 1.

To add or subtract decimals, first **align,** or line up, the decimal points. Then add or subtract the same way you do whole numbers.

This table shows the sales amounts a department store earned each quarter.

DEPARTMENT STORE'S SALES AMOUNTS

Quarter	Sales (millions of $)
1	3.39
2	2.7
3	2.05
4	4.265

What are the total sales for all four quarters?

Write a vertical addition problem, with numbers lined up from top to bottom. Be sure to align all decimal points. Use zeros as placeholders if necessary. Then add.

3.39**0**
2.70**0** } **0's as placeholders**
2.05**0**
+4.265
12.405

The total sales are $12.405 million.

How much greater were sales in quarter 4 than in quarter 1?

Write a vertical subtraction problem using the amounts from quarter 1 and quarter 4. Align the decimal points. Then subtract.

4.265
−3.39**0** ← **0 as placeholder**
0.875

Sales in quarter 4 were $0.875 million greater than sales in quarter 1.

SAMPLE At a sports event, Luke scored 8.65 points. Mel scored 9.2 points. How many more points did Mel score than Luke?

A   0.45   B   0.55   C   1.45   D   1.55

The correct answer is B. First write a vertical subtraction problem. Align the decimal points and add 0 as a placeholder after the digit 2 in 9.2. Then subtract. Mel scored 0.55 more points than Luke. Choices A and C are not correct because smaller digits were subtracted from larger digits. Choice D is not correct because 1 was not borrowed from 9.

$$\begin{array}{r} \overset{\;\;\;\;11}{8\ \cancel{9}\ 10} \\ \cancel{9}.\cancel{2}\cancel{0} \\ -8.65 \\ \hline 0.55 \end{array}$$

1 Darnell adds 123.6 and 3.952. Which digit in 3.952 should be aligned with the digit 6 in 123.6?

A   2   C   5

B   3   D   9

2 Which is the most reasonable estimate for the sum 61.92 + 174.8?

A   about 80   C   about 300

B   about 230   D   about 790

3 Tina jogged 2.3 miles Friday and 0.85 mile Sunday. How far did she jog both days?

A   2.15 miles   C   3.15 miles

B   2.55 miles   D   10.8 miles

4 A triathlon consists of a 3.86-kilometer swim, a 180.25-kilometer bike ride, and a 42.195-kilometer run. What is the total distance of the triathlon?

A   226.305 km   C   606.06 km

B   261.045 km   D   988.20 km

5 Latasha earned $289 last week. She earned $213.73 this week. How much more did Latasha earn last week than this week?

A $75.27   C $76.37

B $75.37   D $76.73

6 At the beginning of the month, Jerry had $173 in his checking account. During the month, he added $26.40 to the account and took out $106.95. What was the total amount left in Jerry's account at the end of the month?

A $92.45   C $330.05

B $93.55   D $331.95

7 The population of the United States is about 295.7 million people. The population of New Zealand is about 4.035 million people. How much greater is the population of the United States than New Zealand?

A   218.8 million   C   291.735 million

B   291.665 million   D   292.2 million

SAMPLE At the start of the month, Kelly's plant was 8.625 inches tall. By the end of the month, the plant was 10.5 inches tall. How many inches did the plant grow during the month?

Answer _____

✓ To find the number of inches the plant grew, subtract 10.5 − 8.625. First write the subtraction vertically, with the decimal points aligned. Add 0's as placeholders. Then subtract.

The plant grew 1.875 inches.

$$\begin{array}{r} \overset{14\ 9}{}\overset{9\ \ 10\ 10}{\cancel{10.500}} \\ -\ 8.625 \\ \hline 1.875 \end{array}$$

8 An apartment has two bedrooms. The area of one bedroom is 165.625 square feet. The area of the other bedroom is 156.25 square feet. What is the total area, in square feet, of both bedrooms? Show your work.

Answer _____

9 In a long jump competition, Alex jumped 9.75 feet on her first try and 11 feet on her second try. How many more feet did Alex jump on her second try than on her first try? Show your work.

Answer _____

10 Neil and Ryan subtracted the numbers 16.83 and 2.154. Neil got an answer of 4.71. Ryan got an answer of 14.676. Who got the correct answer, Neil or Ryan? Explain how you know.

_____

_____

11 This table shows the earnings a movie made during its first four weeks in movie theaters.

MOVIE EARNINGS

Week	Money Earned (millions of $)
1	2.06
2	1.257
3	0.993
4	0.77

Part A Write a vertical addition problem that can be used to find the total money earned, in millions of dollars, by this movie during these four weeks.

Be sure to align the decimal points and add 0's as placeholders where needed.

Part B What was the total money earned, in millions of dollars, by this movie during these four weeks? Show your work above.

Answer _____

Multiplying and Dividing Decimals

6.NS.3

When multiplying decimals, it is not necessary to align the decimal points or add zeros as placeholders.

You can estimate to check the reasonableness of your answers.

To multiply decimals, first multiply the numbers as if they were whole numbers. Then count the number of digits after the decimal point in each factor. This is the same as the number of digits after the decimal point in the product.

What is the product of 6.5 × 2.74?

Write a vertical multiplication problem, with numbers lined up from top to bottom. Then multiply.

$$
\begin{array}{rl}
2.74 & \leftarrow \quad \text{2 digits after the decimal point} \\
\times 6.5 & \leftarrow \quad + \text{ 1 digit after the decimal point} \\
\hline
1370 & \\
16440 & \\
\hline
17.810 & \leftarrow \quad \text{3 digits after the decimal point}
\end{array}
$$

The product of 6.5 × 2.74 is 17.810.

In a division problem, the **dividend** is the number being divided. The **divisor** is the number that divides. The **quotient** is the answer.

$$
\begin{array}{r}
2.5 \leftarrow \text{Quotient} \\
5\overline{)12.5} \leftarrow \text{Dividend} \\
\uparrow \\
\end{array}
$$

Divisor

Zeros can be added to the end of the dividend if there are not enough places when moving the decimal point to the right.

$4.724\overline{)87.5} = 4724\overline{)87500}$

To divide decimals, follow these steps:

1. Move the decimal point in the divisor the correct number of places to the right to make it a whole number.
2. Move the decimal point in the dividend the same number of places to the right.
3. Divide the numbers as if they were whole numbers.
4. Place the decimal point in the quotient directly above the decimal point in the dividend.

Brianna has $7.50 to spend on trail mix. Trail mix costs $3.75 per pound. How many pounds of trail mix can she buy?

Divide $7.50 by $3.75.

$$
3.75\overline{)7.50} \quad \rightarrow \quad
\begin{array}{r}
2 \\
375\overline{)750} \\
\underline{750} \\
0 \quad \text{Remainder is 0. Stop.}
\end{array}
$$

7.50 ÷ 3.75 = 2   Brianna can buy 2 pounds of trail mix.

SAMPLE The path around a field is 0.6 mile long. Leon walked around the path 4.5 times. How many miles did Leon walk?

A   2.7   B   5.1   C   10.5   D   27

The correct answer is A. First write the problem vertically. Then multiply as you would with whole numbers. A total of 2 digits are after the decimal points in the factors. So, 2 digits should go after the decimal point in the answer. With the correct decimal point placement, the digits 270 become 2.70 = 2.7. Choices B and C are incorrect because addition was used instead of multiplication. Choice D is incorrect because the product contains 2 digits to the left, not the right, of the decimal point.

$$\begin{array}{r} 0.6 \\ \times 4.5 \\ \hline 270 \end{array}$$

1 How many digits should be after the decimal point in the product of 123.89 × 62.57?

A   two   C   four

B   three   D   five

2 Evan multiplied 72.03 × 9.8. Which product shows the correct placement of the decimal point?

A   70.5894   C   7,058.94

B   705.894   D   70,589.4

3 Nobu will find the quotient of 476.2065 ÷ 58.9. How many places should the decimal point in each number move to the right before he divides?

A   one   C   three

B   two   D   four

4 A stack of newspapers is 22.5 inches thick. Each newspaper is 1.25 inches thick. How many newspapers are in the stack?

A   12   C   21

B   18   D   28

5 Cassie earns $11.42 an hour. How much money does she make working 8.5 hours?

A $19.92   C $97.07

B $90.92   D $970.70

6 A utility company charges $0.125 for each kilowatt-hour of electricity used. Pam's electric bill last month totaled $146.30. How many kilowatt-hours of electricity did she use last month?

A   18.2875   C   1,170.4

B   117.04   D   1,828.75

SAMPLE Shawn drove his car 297 miles using 16.5 gallons of gasoline. What is the average number of miles per gallon his car travels?

Answer _____

To find the average number of miles per gallon, divide 297 by 16.5. Since the divisor has 1 digit after the decimal point, move the decimal points in the divisor and dividend 1 place to the right to make the divisor a whole number. Then divide.

$$16.5\overline{)297} = 165\overline{)2970}$$

```
        18
165)2970
    165
   1320
   1320
      0
```

The car travels an average of 18 miles per gallon.

7 A rental car company charges a mileage fee of $0.40 per mile driven. Douglas rented a car and paid a mileage fee of $171.50. How many miles did Douglas drive the rental car? Show your work.

Answer _____

8 Patrice and Marisa multiplied the numbers 0.382 and 7.52. Patrice got an answer of 28.7264. Marisa got an answer of 2.87264. Who got the correct answer, Patrice or Marisa? Explain how you know.

_____

_____

_____

9 This table shows the federal minimum wage amounts during certain past years.

FEDERAL MINIMUM WAGE

Year	Minimum Wage ($)
1960	1.00
1970	1.60
1980	3.10
1990	3.80
2000	5.15
2010	7.25

Part A Ms. Brown earned the federal minimum wage in the year 2000. During that time, she worked 37.5 hours per week. How much money did she earn each week she worked in the year 2000? Show your work.

> How many digits should the product have? Remember to round the product to the nearest cent.

Answer _____

Part B How many times greater was the federal minimum wage in 1990 than in 1970? Show your work.

Answer _____

REVIEW

Operations

Read each problem. Circle the letter of the best answer.

1 Troy read a 216-page book in 9 hours. How many pages did he read each hour?

   A 21   **C** 26

   B 24   **D** 28

2 Which multiplication expression has the same value as $\frac{4}{5} \div \frac{3}{8}$?

   A $\frac{5}{4} \times \frac{8}{3}$ **C** $\frac{5}{4} \times \frac{3}{8}$

   B $\frac{4}{5} \times \frac{3}{8}$ **D** $\frac{4}{5} \times \frac{8}{3}$

3 Alison bought a snack for $3.84. She paid with a $10 bill. What is a reasonable estimate for the amount of change she should get back?

   A $4   **C** $7

   B $6   **D** $14

4 How many digits are to the right of the decimal point in the product of 3.008 × 10.2?

   A one   **C** three

   B two   **D** four

5 A board is $\frac{2}{3}$ yard long. Jeremy cuts the board into 6 equal pieces. How long is each cut piece?

   A $\frac{1}{9}$ yard   **C** $\frac{1}{4}$ yard

   B $\frac{2}{9}$ yard   **D** $\frac{4}{1}$ yard

6 Oranges cost $1.79 a pound. Miguel bought 3.6 pounds of oranges. How much did the oranges cost, to the nearest cent?

   A $5.39   **C** $16.11

   B $6.44   **D** $64.44

7 The area of a rectangle is $1\frac{1}{2}$ square feet. The width of the rectangle is $\frac{3}{5}$ foot. What is the length of the rectangle?

   A $\frac{2}{5}$ foot   **C** $2\frac{1}{10}$ feet

   B $\frac{9}{10}$ foot   **D** $2\frac{1}{2}$ feet

8 What is the quotient of 15.25 ÷ 0.25?

   A 5.1   **C** 51

   B 6.1   **D** 61

9 Gloria will divide 6.0192 by 0.32. How many places to the right should she move the decimal point in the divisor and dividend before she starts to divide?

Answer _____

10 A mother dog weighs 75 pounds. One of her puppies weighs 6 pounds. How many times greater is the mother dog's weight than her puppy's weight?

Answer _____

11 Which expression has a greater value, $\frac{3}{8} \times \frac{5}{6}$ or $\frac{3}{8} \div \frac{5}{6}$? Explain.

_____

_____

12 What is the sum of 6.04 + 12.6 + 10.619?

Answer _____

13 Vita saved $72 last December. This amount represents $\frac{2}{9}$ of the total amount she saved last year. What is the total amount Vita saved last year?

Answer _____

14 The product of two decimal numbers is 40.392. The first number is 10.8. The second number has the digits 374 but the decimal point is missing. What is the second number, with the decimal point included? Explain how you know.

_____

_____

_____

15 The cost of some paint supplies are shown below.

Paint roller $3.50

Paintbrush $1.75

Paint tray $0.59

Part A What is the cost of one paintbrush, one paint roller, and one paint tray?

Answer _____

Part B Clark bought 2 of each of these items. He paid with a $20 bill. How much change did he get back? Show your work.

Answer _____

16 Jill uses $\frac{3}{4}$ pound of clay to make a piece of pottery.

Part A Write an expression that can be used to find the number of pieces of pottery Jill can make with 12 pounds of clay.

Answer _____

Part B How many pieces of pottery can Jill make with 12 pounds of clay? Explain how you solved this problem.

_____

_____

Factors and Multiples

● **Lesson 1 Greatest Common Factors** reviews what a factor, a common factor, and a greatest common factor are and how to identify them from a set of numbers.

● **Lesson 2 Least Common Multiples** reviews what a multiple, a common multiple, and a least common multiple are and how to identify them from a set of numbers.

Greatest Common Factors

6.NS.4

Numbers that divide into another number without a remainder are factors of that number.

$15 \div 3 = 5$
$15 \div 4 = 3 \text{ R3}$

3 is a factor of 15, but 4 is not.

Every whole number has the factors 1 and itself.

If two or more whole numbers have no factors in common greater than 1, the GCF of the numbers is 1.

The GCF of 15 and 28 is 1.

If one number is a factor of another number, the GCF of the two numbers is the smaller number.

The GCF of 9 and 36 is 9.

Factors are whole numbers that multiply to form a product. For example, factors of 15 are 1, 3, 5, and 15.

A **common factor** is a factor that two or more whole numbers share.

What are the common factors of 36 and 48?

Find the factors of 36 and 48.

Factors of 36: 1, 2, 3, 4, 6, 9, 12, 18, and 36
Factors of 48: 1, 2, 3, 4, 6, 8, 12, 16, 24, and 48

Identify the factors that are the same for both numbers. The factors 1, 2, 3, 4, 6, and 12 are common factors of 36 and 48.

The largest of the common factors between two or more numbers is the **greatest common factor** (GCF).

A summer camp has 16 counselors and 72 campers. The counselors and campers will be divided into groups of equal size. Each group will have the same number of counselors and the same number of campers. What is the greatest number of groups that can be formed?

List the factors of each number.

Factors of 16: 1, 2, 4, 8, and 16
Factors of 72: 1, 2, 3, 4, 6, 8, 9, 12, 18, 24, 36, and 72

The common factors of 16 and 72 are 1, 2, 4, and 8.
The GCF is 8.

The greatest number of groups that can be formed is 8.

SAMPLE A jeweler makes necklaces using red and blue beads. The jeweler has 64 red beads and 112 blue beads. What is the greatest number of identical necklaces the jeweler can make if all the beads are used?

A 8 **B** 16 **C** 24 **D** 32

The correct answer is B. To find the greatest number of necklaces, find the GCF of 64 and 112. To do this, first list the factors of each number.

64: **1, 2, 4, 8, 16,** 32, and 64
112: **1, 2, 4,** 7, **8,** 14, **16,** 28, 56, and 112

The common factors are 1, 2, 4, 8, and 16. Of these, 16 is the greatest.

1 What are all the factors of 18?

A 2, 3, 6, and 9

B 2, 3, 4, 6, 8, and 9

C 1, 2, 3, 6, 9, and 18

D 1, 2, 3, 4, 6, 8, 9, and 18

2 What is the GCF of 45 and 54?

A 3 **C** 8

B 6 **D** 9

3 What factors are common to 10 and 25?

A 1 only **C** 1 and 5

B 5 only **D** 1, 2, and 5

4 The GCF of two numbers is 15. One of the numbers is 75. Which of the following could be the other number?

A 60 **C** 125

B 100 **D** 150

5 Which pair of numbers has a GCF of 8?

A 32 and 36 **C** 48 and 80

B 32 and 48 **D** 56 and 96

6 Silvia has 20 tomato plants and 30 bean plants. She wants to put the plants in rows so that each row has the same number of tomato plants and the same number of bean plants. What is the greatest number of rows Silvia can plant?

A 2 **C** 10

B 5 **D** 20

7 A total of 54 oranges, 81 pears, and 90 apples will be put into gift baskets. Each gift basket will have the same number of oranges, the same number of pears, and the same number of apples. What is the greatest number of baskets that can be made?

A 9 **C** 27

B 18 **D** 54

SAMPLE A gameboard is 24 inches wide and 40 inches long. Square tiles are placed on the gameboard so that none overlap and they cover the gameboard completely. How long is the side length of the largest square tile that can be used on this gameboard?

Answer _____

✓ To find the length of the largest square tile, find the GCF of 24 and 40. Factors of 24 are **1, 2,** 3, **4,** 6, **8,** 12, and 24. Factors of 40 are **1, 2, 4,** 5, **8,** 10, 20, and 40. Of the factors common to both numbers, 8 is the greatest. So, the largest square tile has a side length of 8 inches.

8 Can the GCF of a pair of numbers ever equal one of the numbers? Explain how you know.

_____

_____

9 Write a pair of numbers that has a GCF of 1.

Answer _____

10 What is the greatest common factor of 108 and 132?

Answer _____

11 Three groups of people buy museum tickets. Each museum ticket costs the same amount. The total cost of the tickets for the three groups is $96, $144, and $160. What is the greatest possible price for each museum ticket?

Answer _____

12 An art teacher has 120 colored pencils and 144 markers. He divides the colored pencils and markers into boxes so that each box has the same number of colored pencils and the same number of markers.

Part A What is the greatest number of boxes the art teacher can make?

Answer _____

Part B The art teacher has 60 tubes of paint. He puts the paint in the boxes with the colored pencils and the markers so that each box has the same number of tubes of paint. The art teacher thinks that since 60 is a factor of 120, the greatest number of boxes the he can make will be the same as in part A. Is the art teacher's thinking correct? Explain how you know.

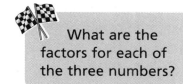

What are the factors for each of the three numbers?

_____

_____

_____

Least Common Multiples

6.NS.4

There is no limit to the number of multiples a number can have.

A **multiple** of a number is the product of that number and a nonzero whole number.

Multiples of 7 are 7, 14, 21, 28, …
since $7 \times 1 = 7$, $7 \times 2 = 14$, $7 \times 3 = 21$, $7 \times 4 = 28$, …

A **common multiple** is a multiple that two or more whole numbers share.

What are the first three common multiples of 6 and 8?

List some multiples of 6 and 8.

Multiples of 6: 6, 12, 18, 24, 30, 36, 42, 48, 54, 60, 66, 72, …
Multiples of 8: 8, 16, 24, 32, 40, 48, 56, 64, 72, 80, 88, 96, …

Identify the first three multiples that are the same for both numbers.

The multiples 24, 48, and 72 are common multiples of 6 and 8.

The LCM of two or more numbers is useful in combining or comparing fractions. Equivalent fractions can be made by first finding the LCM of the denominators.

If one number is a factor of another number, the LCM of the two numbers is the greater number.
   The LCM of 4 and 16 is 16.

The smallest of the common multiples between two or more numbers is the **least common multiple** (LCM).

Thomas waters his garden every 4 days and weeds his garden every 6 days. He watered and weeded his garden today. What is the fewest number of days before Thomas will water and weed his garden again on the same day?

List the first few multiples of 4 and 6.

Multiples of 4: 4, 8, 12, 16, 20, 24, …
Multiples of 6: 6, 12, 18, 24, 30, …

Find the first number that is a common multiple of 4 and 6. It is 12.

Thomas will water and weed on the same day in 12 days.

SAMPLE Which of the following fractions has the greatest value?

A $\frac{3}{4}$ B $\frac{5}{8}$ C $\frac{7}{12}$ D $\frac{11}{16}$

The correct answer is A. First change each fraction into an equivalent fraction. To do this, find the LCM of the denominators, 4, 8, 12, and 16. Since 4 and 8 are factors of 16, the LCM of 4, 8, and 16 is 16. So you only need to list multiples of 12 and 16. Multiples of 12 are 12, 24, 36, **48**, …. Multiples of 16 are 16, 32, **48**, 64, …. The LCM is 48. This becomes the denominator for each equivalent fraction: $\frac{3 \times 12}{4 \times 12} = \frac{36}{48}, \frac{5 \times 6}{8 \times 6} = \frac{30}{48}, \frac{7 \times 4}{12 \times 4} = \frac{28}{48}, \frac{11 \times 3}{16 \times 3} = \frac{33}{48}$.

Finally, compare numerators to find the fraction with the greatest value. The largest numerator is 36, so $\frac{3}{4}$ has the greatest value.

1 What are all the first five multiples of 40?

A   2, 4, 5, 8, and 10

B   10, 20, 40, 80, and 120

C   40, 60, 80, 100, and 120

D   40, 80, 120, 160, and 200

2 What is the LCM of the denominators for $\frac{3}{16}$ and $\frac{3}{10}$?

A   40   C   80

B   60   D   160

3 What are the first three common multiples of 9 and 15?

A   15, 30, and 45

B   45, 90, and 135

C   90, 150, and 180

D   135, 270, and 405

4 Two cruise ships sail from New York to Florida. One ship makes the round trip in 8 days. The other ship makes the round trip in 10 days. Both ships sail from New York today. What is the fewest number of days before both ships will sail again from New York on the same day?

A   10   C   40

B   18   D   80

5 Which pair of numbers has a LCM of 24?

A   6 and 12   C   24 and 48

B   6 and 24   D   24 and 96

6 During a grand opening, a movie theater gives a free ticket to every 25th customer and a free popcorn to every 40th customer. Which customer will be the first to receive both a free ticket and a free popcorn?

A   100th   C   400th

B   200th   D   500th

SAMPLE What are three numbers whose LCM is 100?

Answer _____

For any set of numbers, if one number is a factor of another, the larger number is the LCM. Some factors of 100 are 10 and 25. So three numbers whose LCM is 100 include the two factors 10 and 25 as well as 100 itself.

7 List the fractions $\frac{5}{6}$, $\frac{5}{8}$, and $\frac{7}{10}$ in order from least to greatest.

Answer _____

8 What is the least common multiple of 36 and 48?

Answer _____

9 A clock chimes every 60 minutes. A siren whistles every 90 minutes. What is the fewest number of minutes between the time the clock chimes and the siren whistles together at the same time?

Answer _____

10 Plastic spoons come in boxes of 15. Plastic forks come in boxes of 20. Eliza wants to buy the same number of plastic spoons as plastic forks. What is the least number of each box she can buy?

Answer _____

11 This diagram shows multiples of 6 and multiples of 10.

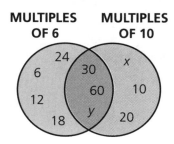

MULTIPLES   MULTIPLES
OF 6   OF 10

24   30   x
6   10
          60
12   y   20
18

The section that overlaps in the middle shows common multiples of 6 and 10.

Part A What is a possible value for *x* in this diagram? Explain how you know.

_____

_____

Part B What is a possible value for *y* in this diagram? Explain how you know.

_____

_____

_____

What are the common multiples of 6 and 10? It may help to make a list of multiples for each number.

REVIEW

Factors and Multiples

Read each problem. Circle the letter of the best answer.

1 What are all the factors of 42?

A 2, 6, 7, 21

B 2, 3, 6, 7, 14, 21

C 1, 2, 3, 4, 11, 21, 42

D 1, 2, 3, 6, 7, 14, 21, 42

2 What are the first four multiples of 8?

A 1, 2, 4, 8   **C** 8, 16, 24, 32

B 2, 4, 8, 16   **D** 8, 18, 28, 38

3 What are the common factors of 50 and 60?

A 2, 5, and 10

B 1, 2, 5, and 10

C 1, 2, 4, 5, 10, and 20

D 1, 2, 5, 10, 20, and 25

4 What is the greatest common factor of 32, 48, and 60?

A 4   **C** 8

B 6   **D** 12

5 Donna goes to the gym every 2 days. Rita goes every 3 days. They both went to the gym on May 1. What is the next day Donna and Rita will go to the gym on the same day?

A May 3   **C** May 6

B May 4   **D** May 7

6 What is the LCM of 80 and 120?

A 120   **C** 240

B 160   **D** 320

7 There are 12 adult and 30 teen volunteers for a park clean-up day. The volunteers will be divided into equal sized groups. Each group will have the same number of adults and the same number of teens. What is the greatest number of groups that can be formed?

A 6   **C** 12

B 8   **D** 30

8 Which pair of numbers has an LCM of 21?

A 3 and 7   **C** 42 and 84

B 21 and 42   **D** 63 and 84

9 What are the first three common multiples of 20 and 25?

Answer _____

10 Write a pair of numbers that has a GCF of 9.

Answer _____

11 Small envelopes come in boxes of 100. Long envelopes come in boxes of 75. Philip wants the same number of each type of envelope. What is the least number of each type of envelope Philip will need to get?

Answer _____

12 Jen, Mia, and Bart each earn the same hourly rate. One week, Jen earned a total of $180, Mia earned a total of $270, and Bart earned a total of $300. What is the greatest possible hourly rate they can earn?

Answer _____

13 What is the LCM of 9, 12, and 15?

Answer _____

14 Two trains leave a station at the same time. One train returns to the station in 45 minutes and leaves again. The other train returns in 75 minutes and leaves again. After how many minutes will both trains return to the station at the same time?

Answer _____

15 Can a pair of numbers ever have a GCF of 1? Explain how you know.

_____

_____

16 A daily newspaper prints a special town feature every 4 days and a special coupon insert every 6 days. Today, both the town feature and the coupon insert are printed.

Part A In how many days will both the town feature and the coupon insert be printed on the same day?

Answer _____

Part B Today is June 1. There are 30 days in June. What are the next three dates that both the town feature and the coupon insert will be printed on the same day?

Answer _____

17 Peanuts come in 36-ounce packages. Raisins come in 16-ounce packages. Nick wants to mix the peanuts with the raisins so that each mixture has the same number of ounces of peanuts and the same number of ounces of raisins.

Part A Can a total of 2 mixtures be made with one package each of the peanuts and raisins? Explain how you know.

_____

_____

Part B What is the greatest number of mixtures of peanuts and raisins that Nick can make with one package of each?

Answer _____

Positive and Negative Numbers

- **Lesson 1 Integers** reviews what an integer is and situations when they are used.

- **Lesson 2 Rational Numbers on Number Lines** reviews what an opposite is and how numbers lines are used to show integers and other rational numbers.

- **Lesson 3 Coordinate Graphing** reviews integers on a coordinate plane and how to identify and plot points on a coordinate plane.

- **Lesson 4 Comparing Integers** reviews using number lines and inequality symbols to compare and order integers.

- **Lesson 5 Absolute Value** reviews what an absolute value is and how it relates to number lines and integers.

Integers

6.NS.5

Whole numbers include 0 and the counting numbers.

0, 1, 2, 3, 4, …

Some key words that help show situations involving positive and negative numbers are

Positive (+)
  above
  deposit
  profit
  increase

Negative (–)
  below
  withdraw
  loss
  decrease

Positive integers can be written with or without a + sign. Their value is the same.

+8 = 8

Negative integers must have the – sign in front of the number.

An **integer** is a whole number or its opposite. It can be positive, negative, or zero.

A **positive integer** is an integer greater than 0. Positive integers include 1, 2, 3, 4, 5, ….

A **negative integer** is an integer less than 0. Negative integers include –1, –2, –3, –4, –5, ….

Positive and negative integers can be used to describe situations in everyday life.

The temperature reading on this thermometer shows –15° Fahrenheit.

What integer describes this temperature?

A temperature of –15°F is represented by the integer –15.

Sandy received the check shown below.

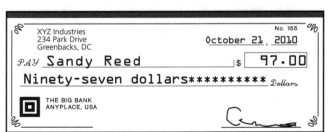

What integer describes the amount of this check?

As a whole number, ninety-seven is represented by 97. Since the check is for Sandy, it represents a positive amount, so the integer represented is +97, or 97.

UNIT 4 :::
Positive and Negative Numbers

SAMPLE Which situation can best be described using a negative integer?

    A   35 dollar deposit   **C**   200 feet above sea level

    B   5 points under par   **D**   2 degree temperature increase

> The correct answer is B. Look for key words in each situation that describe the value of the number. Key words in each answer include: *deposit* in A, *under* in B, *above* in C, and *increase* in D. The words *deposit, above,* and *increase* all refer to positive amounts. Only *under* refers to a negative amount.

1 Which of the following numbers is a negative integer?

    A   -4.5   **C**   0

    B   -59   **D**   3

2 What number represents a refrigerator temperature of 40°F?

    A   -40   **C**   4

    B   -4   **D**   40

3 Sam earned $11 recycling aluminum cans. What integer represents this amount?

    A   11   **C**   1,100

    B   -11   **D**   -1,100

4 What integer represents a distance of 95 feet below sea level?

    A   9.5   **C**   95

    B   -9.5   **D**   -95

5 Catherine received a $750 bonus. What integer best represents this situation?

    A   7.50   **C**   750

    B   -7.50   **D**   -750

6 Which situation is best represented by the integer +8?

    A   8 years ago   **C** $8 payment

    B   8-yard gain   **D**   8-hour delay

7 The title of a newspaper article shows "Company reports a two-million-dollar loss." What integer represents this situation?

    A   -2,000,000   **C**   2

    B   -2   **D**   2,000,000

8 A sign on a store window shows "ten thousand dollar winning lottery ticket sold here." What integer represents this situation?

    A   -10,000   **C**   10

    B   -10   **D**   10,000

SAMPLE All tents at a sporting goods store are on sale for $25 off. What integer represents this situation?

Answer _____

 The key word in this situation is *off*. This indicates a decrease in value which is represented by a negative number. So, a sale of $25 off is represented by the integer -25.

9 Which of the following numbers are integers?

$\frac{7}{2}$ -6 $\frac{2}{3}$ 1.5   1,536 $-\frac{1}{4}$ -900

Answer _____

10 Is 0 a positive integer? Explain how you know.

_____

_____

11 Describe a situation that can be represented by the number -78.

_____

_____

12 Cole and his band made an album. Last month, he made a profit of twelve hundred dollars on the sale of the album. What integer can be used to represent this situation?

Answer _____

13 A part of Rhonda's checkbook record is shown below.

Date	Description	Amount	Total
August 1	Beginning balance	$274	$274
August 8	Paycheck deposit	$185	
August 15	Cash withdrawal	$100	
August 20	Bill payment withdrawal	$52	
August 23	Birthday gift deposit	$75	

Part A What integer can be used to represent the dollar amount entered on August 8? Explain how you know.

_____

_____

Part B Which day or days in the checkbook record can be represented by a negative integer? Explain how you know.

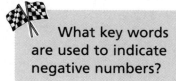

What key words are used to indicate negative numbers?

_____

_____

_____

Rational Numbers on Number Lines

6.NS.6.a, c

0 is the only integer that is its own opposite. 0 is neither positive nor negative.

A rational number can be expressed as a ratio.

$$0.25 = \frac{1}{4} \qquad -4 = -\frac{4}{1}$$

Positive integers can be written with or without a + sign. The value is the same.

$$+8 = 8$$

Negative integers must have the – sign in front of the number.

Distance is always measured in positive units.

The integers –15 and +15 are both 15 units from 0 on a number line.

Integers include whole numbers and their opposites. **Opposites** are the same distance from 0. The integers –3 and +3 are opposites because they are both 3 units from 0.

Write the opposites of 5 and –9.

5 and –5 are both 5 units from 0. So, –5 is the opposite of 5.

–9 and +9 are both 9 units from 0. +9 is the opposite of –9.

A number line can show the location of integers and other **rational numbers.** On a number line, opposites are the same distance from 0 but on different sides of 0.

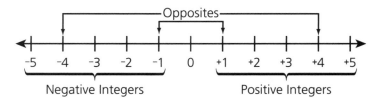

A number line is shown below.

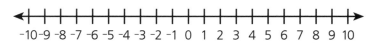

Use this number line to graph +7 and its opposite.

The opposite of +7 is –7 since both numbers are 7 units from 0 on the number line.

UNIT 4
Positive and Negative Numbers

SAMPLE What is the opposite of the opposite of 6?

A 6   B $\frac{1}{6}$ C -6   D -$\frac{1}{6}$

The correct answer is A. You are asked to find the opposite of an opposite. The opposite of 6 is -6. The opposite of this opposite is -(-6). This is the same as -1 × -6 = +6. So, the opposite of an opposite is the original number itself.

1 What is the distance from -50 to 0 on a number line?

A 5 units   C -5 units

B 50 units   D -50 units

2 Which number line shows the opposite of -2?

A

B
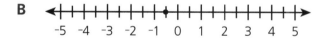

C
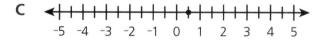

D

3 Which number is the same distance as 10 from 0 on a number line?

A $\frac{1}{10}$ C 20

B -10   D 100

4 How many units from 0 is the point shown on this number line?

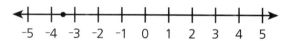

A -3.5   C 35

B -35   D 3.5

5 What is the opposite of the opposite of -8?

A -8   C $\frac{1}{8}$

B -$\frac{1}{8}$ D 8

6 Which number represents the opposite of -25?

A -25   C -(-25)

B -(+25)   D +(-25)

7 What is the opposite of the number shown on this number line?

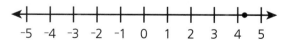

A $4\frac{1}{4}$ C -42

B 42   D -$4\frac{1}{4}$

SAMPLE Which number is the opposite of the number represented by the letter *X* on this number line?

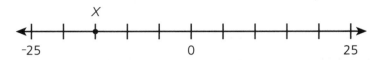

Answer _____

First identify the scale used on the number line There are 5 tick marks between -25 and 0 and between 0 and 25. So, each tick mark represents 25 ÷ 5 = 5 units. Next, identify the location of *X*. It is 3 tick marks from the left of 0, so its value is -3 × 5 = -15. The opposite of -15 is +15.

8 What is the opposite of -7.4?

Answer _____

9 Kyle wrote a number, *n*. Vern wrote the opposite of *n*. Kyle and Vern wrote the same number. What is the number they wrote? Explain how you know.

_____

_____

10 The opposite of the opposite of a number is -100. What is the number?

Answer _____

11 Use this number line to graph the number 4 and its opposite.

12 This diagram compares the elevations, in meters, of some of the
tallest buildings in Washington, D.C., with some of the lowest
locations in the world.

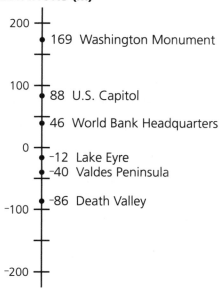

ELEVATIONS (m)

200

169 Washington Monument

100

88 U.S. Capitol

46 World Bank Headquarters

0

-12 Lake Eyre

-40 Valdes Peninsula

-86 Death Valley

-100

-200

Part A What number represents the opposite of the elevation
of Lake Eyre?

Answer _____

Part B Which Washington, D.C., building is closest in height to
the opposite of one of the lowest elevations shown in
the diagram? Explain how you know.

What is the
opposite of each
building height?
Which opposite is
closest to a labeled
low elevation?

_____

_____

_____

Coordinate Graphing

6.NS.6.b, c; 6.NS.8

You can think of the *x*- and *y*-axes as horizontal and vertical number lines that overlap.

The ordered pair that represents the origin is (0, 0).

If an *x*-coordinate is positive, move right. If it is negative, move left. If a *y*-coordinate is positive, move up. If it is negative, move down.

A coordinate plane is divided into four regions, called **quadrants.**

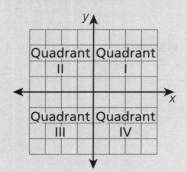

Roman numerals (I, II, III, and IV) are used to name the quadrants.

A **coordinate plane** has a horizontal axis and a vertical axis. The horizontal axis is called the **x-axis.** The vertical axis is called the **y-axis.** Both axes contain the positive integers, the negative integers, and 0.

A coordinate plane is used to locate points. **Ordered pairs** name the location of the points. Each ordered pair has two numbers, such as (3, –2). The first number is the **x-coordinate.** It tells you how far to move left or right from the center, or **origin,** of the coordinate plane. The second number is the **y-coordinate.** It tells you how far to move up or down from the first number.

Graph the point (3, –2) on a coordinate plane.

The first number, 3, tells you how far to move left or right, along the *x*-axis. Since 3 is positive, move right 3 units.

The second number, –2, tells you how far to move up or down from the first number. Since –2 is negative, move down 2 units.

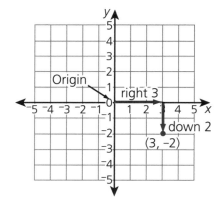

UNIT 4
Positive and Negative Numbers

SAMPLE Which of the following points is located in quadrant III?

     A (3, 5)   **B** (−1, 6)   **C** (2, −5)   **D** (−4, −3)

The correct answer is D. Quadrant III is located in the lower left region of a coordinate plane.

In this region, the *x*-coordinates and the *y*-coordinates are both negative. The only given ordered pair with two negative coordinates is (−4, −3).

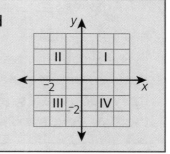

---

1 Triangle *QRS* is shown on this coordinate plane.

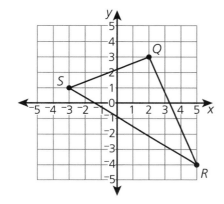

What is the *y*-coordinate of point *R*?

  A 5   **C** −3

  B 3   **D** −4

2 Which quadrant is the point (8, 4) located in?

  A quadrant I   **C** quadrant III

  B quadrant II   **D** quadrant IV

3 Which point lies on the *x*-axis?

  A (0, 2)   **C** (2, 2)

  B (2, 0)   **D** (−2, −2)

4 Square *ABCD* is shown on this coordinate plane.

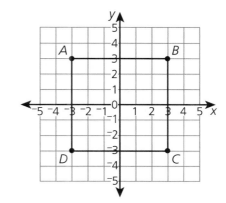

Which point has the coordinates (3, −3)?

  A point *A*   **C** point *C*

  B point *B*   **D** point *D*

5 Which statement is true of any point located in quadrant II of a coordinate plane?

  A Only the *x*-coordinate is positive.

  B Only the *y*-coordinate is positive.

  C Both *x*- and *y*-coordinates are positive.

  D Neither *x*- nor *y*-coordinates are positive.

SAMPLE What is the distance between the points (–2, 3) and (–2, 9) on a coordinate plane?

Answer _____

   The *x*-coordinates of both points are the same. So, to find the distance between the points, simply find the difference between the *y*-coordinates of each point: $9 - 3 = 6$. The distance between the two points is 6 units.

6 Graph the point (4, –1) on the coordinate plane below.

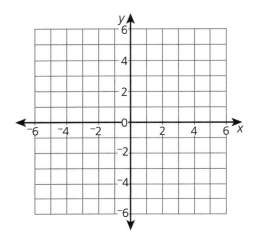

7 Felicia tried to graph the point (5, 1) on the coordinate plane at the right.

What mistake did she make?
Explain how you know.

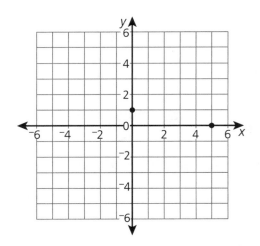

_____

_____

UNIT 4 :::
Positive and Negative Numbers

8 This coordinate plane represents a map of some towns in Hillsboro County.

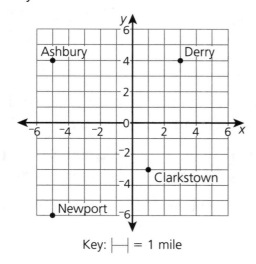

Key: $\vdash\!\!\dashv$ = 1 mile

Part A What coordinates represent the location of Clarkstown?

Answer _____

Part B What is the distance, in miles, between Ashbury and Derry? Explain how you know.

> First identify the ordered pairs representing the location of each town. How can you find the distance between the points?

_____

_____

Comparing Integers

6.NS.7.a, b

Numbers to the left on a number line are smaller than numbers on the right.

Inequality symbols are sometimes used to order integers.

Use < to order from least to greatest.

Use > to order from greatest to least.

More than one < or more than one > can be used in a single inequality statement.

-15 < -3 < 5

-2 > -6 > -9

A number line can be used to compare integers. The **inequality symbols** below are used to show the comparisons.

is less than (<)   **is greater than (>)**
is less than or equal to (≤)   **is greater than or equal to (≥)**

What inequality symbol makes this comparison correct?

-2 ☐ -6

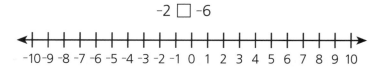

On the number line, -2 is to the right of -6. Since numbers to the right are larger than numbers on the left, -2 is greater than -6.

-2 > -6 or -2 ≥ -6

A number line can also be used to order integers. They can be ordered from least to greatest or from greatest to least.

Order the integers -5, -8, 0, and -1 from least to greatest.

Locate each integer on a number line.

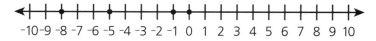

From the number line, you can see than -8 is farthest left, so it is the smallest number. 0 is farthest right, so it is the largest.

The numbers, in order from least to greatest, are -8, -5, -1, and 0.

SAMPLE Which inequality statement correctly orders the integers –11, –16, and –14 from greatest to least?

A $-11 < -16 < -14$

C $-11 > -16 > -14$

B $-11 < -14 < -16$

D $-11 > -14 > -16$

The correct answer is D. The is-greater-than symbol, >, is used to order from greatest to least. Since choices A and B use the is-less-than symbol, they are incorrect. Draw a number line and locate the given integers.

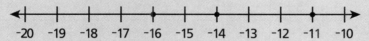

Numbers to the right on a number line are greater than numbers on the left, so $-11 > -14 > -16$.

1 Abby scored –4 in a game. Trudy scored 3, Melanie scored –5, and Gia scored –2. Who received the score with the lowest value?

A Abby

C Melanie

B Trudy

D Gia

2 Which inequality statement is true?

A $-6 \geq 0$

C $-5 \geq -1$

B $-3 \geq 1$

D $-4 \geq -7$

3 Use this number line to help answer the question.

Which inequality statement is true?

A $-7 < -4 < -2$

C $-4 < -7 < -2$

B $-7 > -4 > -2$

D $-4 > -7 > -2$

4 Which comparison does the symbol < make correct?

A $8 \square 3$

C $-7 \square -1$

B $4 \square -6$

D $-2 \square -5$

5 Which statement is true?

A $-28 \geq -26$

C $-36 \leq -39$

B $-33 \geq -29$

D $-46 \leq -37$

6 The temperature at 1:00 was –7°. At 4:00, it was –12°. At 6:00, it was –9°. Which statement is true?

A It was warmer at 1:00 than at 4:00.

B It was warmer at 4:00 than at 6:00.

C It was colder at 1:00 than at 4:00.

D It was colder at 6:00 than at 4:00.

SAMPLE The approximate depths of some oceans are shown in the table below.

Ocean	Depth (ft)
Atlantic	-30,246
Indian	-24,460
Pacific	-35,837

Write an inequality statement to list the numbers in order from least to greatest.

Answer _____

On a number line, the number that is farthest left is -35,837. This is the smallest of the numbers. The number that is farthest right is -24,460. This is the largest number. The number -30,246 falls between. So the order, from least to greatest, is -35,837 < -30,246 < -24,460.

7 Use inequality symbols, < or >, to list the integers 4, -1, 2, and -5 in order.

Answer _____

8 Write an integer that is greater than -53 but less than -49.

Answer _____

9 Gary thinks the statement 0 < -62 is true. Explain whether or not Gary is correct.

_____

_____

10 The balance amounts in a small business bank account for the month of May are shown in the table below.

Day	Balance ($)
May 1	-83
May 3	-235
May 4	55
May 6	-181
May 13	-64
May 20	-152
May 24	-40
May 26	225

Part A Which days had a balance greater than on May 1?

Answer _____

How can you tell if a number is larger or smaller than -83?

Part B For the days May 20, May 24, and May 26, list the balance amounts, in dollars, in order from greatest to least. Explain how you can use a number line to help you find your answer.

_____

_____

_____

Absolute Value

6.NS.7.c, d

The **absolute value** of a number is its distance from 0 on a number line. The symbols │ │ are used to show absolute value.

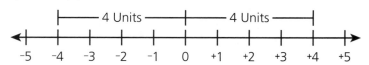

$|4| = 4$ since 4 is 4 units from 0.

$|{-}4| = 4$ since -4 is also 4 units from 0.

Which two numbers have an absolute value equal to 32?

The numbers that have an absolute value of 32 are 32 units from 0 on a number line. One number is +32. The other number is its opposite, -32.

$$|32| = 32 \text{ and } |{-}32| = 32$$

Absolute values can be used to model real-world situations.

In the first play of a football game, the Bears gained a distance of 14 yards. In the second play, they lost a distance of 6 yards. Write absolute value statements to describe the distance traveled in the first play and the distance traveled in the second play.

A gain in yards is represented by a positive number inside the absolute value symbols.

$$|14| = 14 \text{ yards traveled in the first play}$$

A loss in yards is represented by a negative number inside the absolute value symbols.

$$|{-}6| = 6 \text{ yards traveled in the second play}$$

The positive result, 6, of the absolute value shows there was a change in distance of 6 yards.

$|4|$ is read as "the absolute value of 4."

$|{-}4|$ is read as "the absolute value of negative 4."

Any number and its opposite have the same absolute value.

$$|598| = 598$$
$$|{-}598| = 598$$

The absolute value of any number is always positive or zero. Absolute values are never negative.

UNIT 4 ✖✖
Positive and Negative Numbers

Read each problem. Circle the letter of the best answer.

SAMPLE What is the value of the expression $-|-12|$?

      A 12   **B** -12   **C** 0 or 12   **D** 12 or -12

The correct answer is B. This expression asks you to find the opposite of $|-12|$. The absolute value of any number is always positive, so $|-12| = 12$. The opposite of 12 is -12, so $-|-12| = -12$.

---

1 Use this number line to help answer the question.

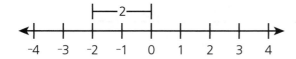

Which statement is modeled by this number line?

  A $-2 = 2$ **C** $|2| = -2$

  B $|2| = 2$ **D** $|-2| = 2$

2 Malik threw a round flying disk forward. Because of a strong wind, the disk landed 10 feet behind him. Which absolute value statement can be used to model the distance the flying disk traveled?

  A $|10| = -10$ **C** $|-10| = -10$

  B $|-10| = 10$ **D** $-|-10| = 10$

3 Use this number line to help answer the question.

Which numbers have an absolute value of 5?

  A 5 only   **C** 5 and -5

  B -5 only   **D** 0, 5, and -5

4 Use this number line to help answer the question.

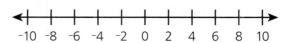

Which statement is true?

  A $-|6| = -6$ **C** $|-7| = -7$

  B $-|-3| = 3$ **D** $-|-9| = 9$

5 The value of d in the inequality below represents the depth, in feet, of a submarine in water.

$$d < -75$$

Which statement best describes d?

  A The depth of the submarine is exactly 75 feet above the water's surface.

  B The depth of the submarine is exactly 75 feet below the water's surface.

  C The depth of the submarine is less than 75 feet below the water's surface.

  D The depth of the submarine is greater than 75 feet below the water's surface.

SAMPLE Paul wrote two checks from his checking account. His account balance is now less than -57 dollars.

Write a statement that describes the size of Paul's debt.

Answer _____

An account balance of -57 represents a debt of $57. An account balance less than -57 dollars could be -58 dollars, -59 dollars, -60 dollars, or any other number of dollars beyond this. These numbers represent debts of $58, $59, $60, or greater. So, Paul's debt is greater than $57.

6 What is the value of the expression $-3|-5|$?

Answer _____

7 What value of *n* makes the statement below true?

$$|0| = n$$

Answer _____

8 Diego thinks $|-40| = -40$. Is his thinking correct? Explain how you know.

_____

_____

9 Aron wrote this expression.

$$|25|$$

Part A What is the value of the expression?

Answer _____

Part B What other absolute value has the same value as $|25|$? Explain how you know.

> Remember that the absolute value of a number is its distance from 0 on a number line. What other number is 25 units from 0 on a number line?

_____

_____

_____

10 On Monday, the value of a stock dropped 4 points.

Part A Write an absolute value statement to model the change in value of the stock on Monday.

Answer _____

Part B By Friday, the value of the stock dropped more than 11 points.

Write an inequality statement that best describes p, the change in points of the stock by Friday.

Answer _____

REVIEW

Positive and Negative Numbers

Read each problem. Circle the letter of the best answer.

1 Which of the following numbers is a negative integer?

   A   0   **C**   14

   B $-\frac{1}{2}$ **D**   –71

2 Which number represents the opposite of –7?

   A   –(7)   **C**   –(–7)

   B   –(+7)   **D**   +(–7)

3 What ordered pair represents the location of point Q on the hiking trail grid below?

HIKING TRAIL

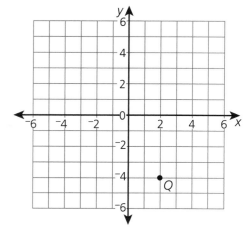

   A   (2, –4)   **C**   (–2, 4)

   B   (–4, 2)   **D**   (4, –2)

4 Which situation can best be described using a positive integer?

   A   10 yards lost

   B   2-inch increase

   C   50 dollars spent

   D   5 degrees below zero

5 What temperature is represented on the thermometer below?

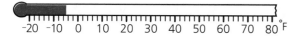

   A   5°F   **C**   –5°F

   B   10°F   **D**   –15°F

6 Which inequality statement is true?

   A   –8 < 0   **C**   –6 < –6

   B   0 < –4   **D**   –7 < –9

7 Which number or numbers have an absolute value of 2?

   A   2 only   **C**   2 and –2

   B   –2 only   **D**   0, 2, and –2

8 Name a point that is located in quadrant IV on a coordinate plane.

Answer _____

9 Jack paid two hundred seventy-five dollars for a new bike. What integer can be used to represent this situation?

Answer _____

10 What is the value of the expression $2|-12|$?

Answer _____

11 The opposite of the opposite of a number is –16. What is the number?

Answer _____

12 Use inequality symbols, $<$ or $>$, and this number line to list the integers –3, 4, –6, and 1 in order from least to greatest.

Answer _____

13 Hiro thinks $-|-5| = -5$. Is Hiro's thinking correct? Explain how you know.

_____

_____

14 Use this number line to graph the opposite of the opposite of –1.

15 Right triangle *RST* is shown on the coordinate plane at the right.

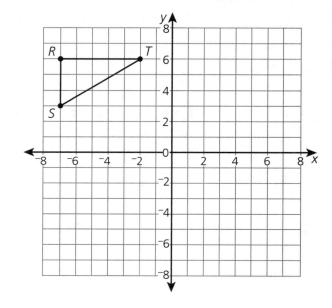

Part A What quadrant is the right triangle located in?

Answer _____

Part B What is the length, in units, of side $\overline{RS}$? Explain how you know.

_____

_____

_____

16 A clock counts down time in seconds. Shortly before the start of a game, the clock reads -60.

Part A Write an absolute value statement to model this amount of time, in seconds, on the clock before the start of the game.

Answer _____

Part B When the clock first starts counting down time, there are more than 300 seconds before the start of the game.

Write an inequality statement that best describes *t*, the time in seconds, when the clock first starts counting down time.

Answer _____

UNIT 4 ▓▓
Positive and Negative Numbers

Expressions

- **Lesson 1 Writing Expressions** reviews how to translate words into numerical and algebraic expressions.

- **Lesson 2 Evaluating Expressions** reviews how to evaluate numerical and algebraic expressions using the correct order of operations.

- **Lesson 3 Operation Properties** reviews equivalent numerical and algebraic expressions as well as the commutative, associative, and distributive properties.

Writing Expressions

6.EE.1; 6.EE.2.a, b

Key words used in translating operations are

(+) add
 sum
 plus
 increased by
 more than
 all together

(−) subtract
 difference
 minus
 fewer
 less than
 decreased by
 take away
 how much more

(×) multiply
 product
 times
 groups of
 in all

(÷) divide
 quotient
 groups of
 share
 split equally

The symbols ×, ( ), or • are used to show multiplication.

A number directly next to a variable in an algebraic expression also indicates multiplication.

6p means 6 × p

Use exponents when you see key words like *squared, cubed,* or *raised to a power.*

An **expression** is a grouping of numbers, symbols, and operations that show the value of something. A **numerical expression** is an expression containing only numbers and operations.

8 + 5 × 3 is a numerical expression.

An **algebraic expression** is an expression that also contains symbols, or letters. These letters, called **variables,** represent values that can change.

Some examples of algebraic expressions include

$$5x \qquad a + b \qquad \frac{2n}{5 + p}$$

You can translate words into numerical expressions.

Baylor earned $45 on Saturday and $63 on Sunday. Write an expression to show how much more money Baylor earned on Sunday than on Saturday.

Look for key words to help you choose what operation to use. The words *how much more* indicate subtraction. Subtract Saturday's earnings from Sunday's to find how much more.

$63 − $45 is the same as the expression 63 − 45.

You can translate words into algebraic expressions.

Lucia wants to buy some CDs. Each CD costs $14. Write an expression to represent Lucy's total cost for *n* CDs.

You need to write an algebraic expression since the number of CDs Lucia will buy is not known. Multiplication is used to find totals when items cost the same amount.

$14 per CD × *n* CDs is the same as the expression 14*n*.

SAMPLE The side length of a square is 7 inches. Each side is increased by 3 inches. Which expression can be used to find the area, in square inches, of the square?

    A $2(7 + 3)$ **B** $2(7 - 3)$ **C** $(7 + 3)^2$ **D** $(7 - 3)^2$

> The correct answer is C. Look for key words to help choose the operation or operations to use. The words *increased by* mean addition. The increased side length is shown by $(7 + 3)$. To find the area of a square, the side length is squared, or raised to the 2nd power. So the expression for the area is $(7 + 3)^2$.

1 Which expression shows the difference between 8 and 2?

    A $8 > 2$ **C** $8 - 2$

    B $8 < 2$ **D** $2 - 8$

2 What expression shows the quotient of 6 and p?

    A $6 \times p$ **C** $p \times 6$

    B $6 \div p$ **D** $p \div 6$

3 The product of 4 and 3 is raised to the 5th power. Which expression shows this?

    A $(4 \times 3)^5$ **C** 4×3^5

    B $\left(\dfrac{4}{3}\right)^5$ **D** $\dfrac{4^5}{3}$

4 Grady now has a total of 81 people in his address book. This week, 9 people were added. Which expression shows the number of people in Grady's address book last week?

    A $81 + 9$ **C** 81×9

    B $81 - 9$ **D** $81 \div 9$

5 Look at the expression below.

    $3w + 5x$

What two terms are being added?

    A 3 and w **C** 3 and 5

    B 5 and x **D** $3w$ and $5x$

6 Which word phrase describes the expression $10 - (6 \div 3)$?

    A the quotient of 10 and the difference between 6 and 3

    B the difference between 10 and the quotient of 6 and 3

    C the quotient of 6 and 3 and the difference between 10

    D the difference between the quotient of 6 and 3 and 10

7 A gym charges a registration fee of $50 and $40 each month for membership. Which expression shows the total cost of m months of membership at the gym?

    A $50 + 40m$ **C** $(50 + 40)m$

    B $50m + 40$ **D** $(50 + 40)^m$

SAMPLE Write an expression to show a number, *n,* less than the product of 8 and 6.

Answer _____

The key words *less than* indicate subtraction. The key word *product* indicates multiplication of 8 and 6, or 8 × 6. Since the number *n* is less than the product, it is subtracted from 8 × 6. The expression is (8 × 6) − *n.*

8 Write an expression to show the product of *x* and (7 + 6).

Answer _____

9 The difference between of 15 and 6 is raised to the 3rd power. What expression shows this?

Answer _____

10 Danielle wrote the expression 32 ÷ (5 + 3). Explain how the expression (5 + 3) can represent a single term or the sum of two terms.

_____

_____

_____

11 Write a word phrase that represents the expression $\frac{3q}{2}$.

Answer _____

12 Sara has a box of 50 charms. She will share them equally among 5 friends. She wants to know how many charms each friend will get.

Part A What are the key words in this situation and what operation do they indicate?

Answer _____

Part B Write an expression that can be used to show how many charms each friend will get.

Answer _____

13 A cube has a side length of 12 inches.

Part A What expression represents the total volume, in cubic inches, of the cube?

Answer _____

The volume of a cube is equal to the cube of the side length. Raising to what power is the same as cubing?

Part B The cube is divided into 4 equal-sized sections. Write an expression to show the volume, in cubic inches, of each section of the cube.

Answer _____

Evaluating Expressions

6.EE.1, 6.EE.2.c

The letters PEMDAS can be used to remember the correct order of operations.

P parentheses
E exponents
M multiplication
D division
A addition
S subtraction

If multiplication and division are in the same expression, do them in the order they appear.

$6 \div 2 \times 3 = 3 \times 3 = 9$

If addition and subtraction are in the same expression, do them in the order they appear.

$12 - 5 + 4 = 7 + 4 = 11$

The expression n^k means n multiplies itself k times.

When $k = 2$, $n^k = n^2$ or $n \times n$.

$5^2 = 5 \times 5 = 25$

When $k = 3$, $n^k = n^3$ or $n \times n \times n$.

$5^3 = 5 \times 5 \times 5 = 125$

To **evaluate** an expression means to find its value. For numerical expressions, perform the operation or operations shown. Be sure to follow the correct **order of operations.**

What is the value of the expression $(12 \div 2) - 3 + 5^2$?

The order of operations says to perform the operations inside parentheses first: $(12 \div 2) = 6$

$$(12 \div 2) - 3 + 5^2 = 6 - 3 + 5^2$$

Next, evaluate the exponent: $5^2 = 25$

$$6 - 3 + 5^2 = 6 - 3 + 25$$

Finally, add and subtract from left to right.

$$6 - 3 + 25 = 3 + 25 = 28$$

The value of $(12 \div 2) - 3 + 5^2$ is 28.

To evaluate algebraic expressions, **substitute,** or replace, each variable in the expression with a numerical value.

The formula $A = \frac{1}{2}(b_1 + b_2)h$ is used to find A, the area of a trapezoid with base lengths b_1 and b_2 and height h.

A trapezoid has base lengths of 8 centimeters and 14 centimeters. Its height is 6 centimeters. What is the area, in square centimeters, of the trapezoid?

To find the area, substitute values for b_1 and b_2 and h into the formula and evaluate using the correct order of operations. In this case, $b_1 = 8$, $b_2 = 14$, and $h = 6$.

$$A = \frac{1}{2}(b_1 + b_2)h$$

$$A = \frac{1}{2}(8 + 14)6 = \frac{1}{2}(22)6 = (11)6 = 66$$

The area of the trapezoid is 66 square centimeters.

SAMPLE What is the value of the expression below when $m = 4$ and $n = 2$?

$$5m - n^3$$

A 12 **B** 14 **C** 26 **D** 28

The correct answer is A. First substitute 4 for m and 2 for n into the expression. This gives $5 \times 4 - 2^3$. Use the correct order of operations to evaluate. Since there are no parentheses, the exponent is done first: $5 \times 4 - 2^3 = 5 \times 4 - 8$. Multiply and then subtract: $5 \times 4 - 8 = 20 - 8 = 12$.

1 The perimeter of a rectangle is given by the expression $2(L + W)$. What is the perimeter of a rectangle when $L = 10$ units and $W = 5$ units?

A 15 units **C** 25 units

B 17 units **D** 30 units

2 Which expression has a value of 16 when $x = 2$?

A $2x$ **C** x^2

B $4x$ **D** x^4

3 What is the missing value in the table below?

n	$n^2 + 1$
0	1
1	2
2	5
3	?

A 7 **C** 10

B 9 **D** 13

4 What is the value of the expression $5 + (6 - 4)^3 \div 2$?

A 5 **C** 8

B 6 **D** 9

5 The formula $SA = 4(3)(r^2)$ represents the approximate surface area of a sphere with a radius of r centimeters. What is the approximate surface area, in square centimeters, of a sphere with a radius of 5 centimeters?

A 70 cm^2 **C** 300 cm^2

B 120 cm^2 **D** 400 cm^2

6 What expression is missing from the table?

n	?
4	16
6	14
8	12
10	10

A $4n$ **C** $n + 12$

B n^2 **D** $20 - n$

SAMPLE What is the value of the expression below?

$$\frac{24 + 4^3}{12 - 4}$$

Answer _____

Use the correct order of operations to evaluate the expression. It is easier to see all operations in a fractional expression when it is rewritten using a division sign: $(24 + 4^3) \div (12 - 4)$. Perform the operations in the parentheses first: $24 + 4^3 = 24 + 64 = 88$ and $12 - 4 = 8$. Finally, divide: $88 \div 8 = 11$.

7 What is the correct order of operations to evaluate the expression below?

$$16 \div (12 - 4) + 2 \times 5$$

Answer _____

8 The volume of a cube-shaped box is given by the expression $(x + 4)^3$. What is the volume of this box when $x = 6$?

Answer _____

9 Kurt evaluated the expression $6^2 - 10$ and got 2. What mistake did Kurt make?

_____

_____

10 Brooke sells bottles of lemonade. The table below shows some amounts of money she receives selling *n* bottles.

BOTTLES OF LEMONADE

Number of Bottles, *n*	Money Received, ($)
6	9
12	18
18	27
24	?

> 🏁 What expression is used to find the cost of *n* bottles of lemonade?

Part A How much money does Brooke receive selling 24 bottles?

Answer _____

Part B How much money does Brooke receive selling 100 bottles? Explain how you know.

_____

_____

_____

11 Apollo will evaluate the expression shown below.

$$100 - (20 \div 5)^2 \times 3$$

Part A What operation should he perform first?

Answer _____

Part B What is the value of this expression? Show your work.

Answer _____

Operation Properties

6.EE.3, 6.EE.4

Many different expressions can be written that are equivalent to each other. Some equivalent expressions for 5*p* are

$$p + p + p + p + p$$
$$6p - p$$
$$2p + 3p$$
$$5p - 4 + 4$$

The commutative property of addition is $a + b = b + a$.

The commutative property of multiplication is $a \cdot b = b \cdot a$.

The associative property of addition is $(a + b) + c = a + (b + c)$.

The associative property of multiplication is $(a \cdot b) \cdot c = a \cdot (b \cdot c)$.

The distributive property of multiplication over addition is $a(b + c) = a \cdot b + a \cdot c$.

The distributive property of multiplication over subtraction is $a(b - c) = a \cdot b - a \cdot c$.

Equivalent expressions are expressions that represent the same value.

$5(2 + 4)$	is equivalent to	$5(6)$
$6x$	is equivalent to	$3x + 3x$
$l + w + l + w$	is equivalent to	$2l + 2w$

Write an expression equivalent to $5y - 2y + 8 - 1$.

You can simplify this to find an equivalent expression. Combine the variable terms and then combine the numerical terms.

$$5y - 2y + 8 - 1 = 3y + 7$$

$3y + 7$ is equivalent to $5y - 2y + 8 - 1$.

Properties of operations are used to make equivalent expressions.

The **commutative property** says you can add or multiply in any order. For example, $4 + 9 = 9 + 4$ and $3 \times 8 = 8 \times 3$. The commutative property does not apply to subtraction or division.

The **associative property** says you can group numbers together using parentheses when you add or multiply. For example, $(1 + 7) + 2 = 1 + (7 + 2)$ and $(4 \times 2) \times 5 = 4 \times (2 \times 5)$. The associative property does not apply to subtraction or division.

The **distributive property** says when you multiply a number by a sum, you can multiply each part of the sum by the number and then add. For example, $2(8 + 5) = 2(8) + 2(5) = 16 + 10 = 26$. The same property applies when multiplying a number by a difference.

Write an expression equivalent to $6(n - 3)$.

Use the distributive property to multiply 6 and the difference between *n* and 3.

$$6(n - 3) = 6(n) - 6(3) = 6n - 18$$

$6n - 18$ is equivalent to $6(n - 3)$.

SAMPLE Which expression is equivalent to $32x - 48y$?

A $6(4x - 8y)$

C $32y - 48x$

B $8(4x - 6y)$

D $48y - 32x$

The correct answer is B. Each term in the expression can be divided by 8: $32x ÷ 8 = 4x$ and $48y ÷ 8 = 6y$. Using the distributive property, $8(4x - 6y) = 32x - 48y$. Choice A is not correct because the wrong number is used to divide. Choice C is not correct because variables alone are not commutative. Choice D is not correct because subtraction is not commutative.

1 Which number sentence shows the commutative property for multiplication?

A $15 \times 9 = 9 \times 15$

B $23 \times 8 = 28 \times 3$

C $6 \times (4 \times 10) = (6 \times 4) \times 10$

D $5 \times (3 \times 7) = (5 \times 3) \times (5 \times 7)$

2 Which value completes the number sentence below?

$$(3 + \square) + 8 = 3 + (2 + 8)$$

A 2

C 5

B 3

D 8

3 Which number sentence is true?

A $j + k = k - j$

C $j - k = k - j$

B $j \times k = k \times j$

D $j ÷ k = k ÷ j$

4 Which expression applies the distributive property to $17(9)$?

A $10(9) + 7(9)$

C $10(10) + 7(1)$

B $10(9) \times 7(9)$

D $10(10) - 7(1)$

5 Which expression is equivalent to $8 + 12n - 4$?

A 16

C $20n - 4$

B $16n$

D $4 + 20n - 8n$

6 Which number sentence is **not** true?

A $7(x - y) = 7x - 7y$

B $2x + 3y + x = 3x + 3y$

C $12x - 10y = 10y - 12x$

D $4x + (5y + 3x) = 4x + (3x + 5y)$

7 Which two expressions have the same value for any x?

A $2x + 3x$ and $6x$

B $x - 8$ and $8 - x$

C $6x(4 - 1)$ and $18x$

D $(x + 5) - 2$ and $x + (5 - 2)$

SAMPLE Which property is represented by the numerical expression below?

$$(6 + 11) + 23 = 23 + (6 + 11)$$

Answer _____

> The commutative property of addition says that $a + b = b + a$. The associative property of addition says that $(a + b) + c = a + (b + c)$. In the number sentence, the entire expression inside the parentheses, $(6 + 11)$, switches order with 23. This represents the commutative property of addition, where $a = 6 + 11$ and $b = 23$.

8 Which property is represented by the number sentence below?

$$(5 \times 4) \times 8 = 5 \times (4 \times 8)$$

Answer _____

9 The expression $2(L + W)$ represents the perimeter of a rectangle. Write an equivalent expression using the distributive property to represent the perimeter of a rectangle.

Answer _____

10 Are the expressions $6x - 2y + 4y$ and $4x + 4y$ equivalent? Explain how you know.

_____

_____

11 A teacher plans to buy the same number of notebooks and rulers for his classroom. Each notebook costs $2. Each ruler costs $1.

Part A Write a numerical expression that represents the total amount of money the teacher will spend on *x* notebooks and *x* rulers.

Which property— associative, commutative, or distributive—could you use to write this expression?

Answer _____

Part B Write an equivalent expression to the one you wrote in part A. Explain how you know it is equivalent.

_____

_____

_____

12 Adam wrote the expression $9 \times (4 \times p)$.

Part A Write an equivalent expression to Adam's expression using the associative property.

Answer _____

Part B Write an equivalent expression to Adam's expression using the commutative property.

Answer _____

REVIEW

Expressions

Read each problem. Circle the letter of the best answer.

1 Which value completes the number sentence $16 + (\square + 13) = 16 + (13 + 3)$?

   A   3   **C**   13

   B   6   **D**   16

2 Which expression shows the quotient of 6 and 12?

   A $6 - 12$ **C** $6 \div 12$

   B $12 - 6$ **D** $12 \div 6$

3 Which number sentence is true?

   A $3(p - q) = 3(q - p)$

   B $3 + (p \times q) = (p \times q) + 3$

   C $(3 + p) - q = 3 + (p - q)$

   D $3 \div (p + q) = (p + q) \div 3$

4 Which expression has a value of 64 when $x = 8$?

   A $2x$ **C** x^2

   B $4x$ **D** x^3

5 Lacy earns $25 each day. So far she earned $350. Which expression can be used to find the number of days Lacy worked?

   A $350 + 25$ **C** 350×25

   B $350 - 25$ **D** $350 \div 25$

6 What two terms are being multiplied in the expression $6(p + 7q)$?

   A   6 and p **C** p and $7q$

   B   7 and q **D**   6 and $p + 7q$

7 Which expression is equivalent to $5x$?

   A $x(9 - 4)$ **C** $5 + x$

   B $x + 2x + 3x$ **D** $5 - 5 - 5x$

8 Which word phrase describes the expression $10 - 2x$?

   A   the sum of 2 and x less than 10

   B   10 less than the sum of 2 and x

   C   the product of 2 and x less than 10

   D   10 less than the product of 2 and x

9 Which property is represented by the number sentence below?

$$(7 \times 8) \times 4 = 4 \times (7 \times 8)$$

Answer _____

10 Write an expression to show the quotient of x^3 and $(2x + 1)$.

Answer _____

11 What is the value of the expression below?

$$\frac{12 + 6^2 \times 2}{6}$$

Answer _____

12 What is the value of the expression $x^2 - 4y$ when $x = 9$ and $y = 2$?

Answer _____

13 Are the expressions $6(4 + 3x)$ and $18x + 24$ equivalent? Explain how you know.

_____

_____

14 Ivan evaluated the expression $8 + 12 \div 2 \times 3$ and got 10. What mistake did he make?

_____

_____

15 The formula for the approximate volume of a sphere with a radius of r feet is $V = \frac{4}{3}(3)(r^3)$. What is the approximate volume, in cubic feet, of a sphere with a radius of 2 feet?

Answer _____

16 Neela wrote this expression.

$$6 \times (n + 5)$$

Part A Write two different expressions that are equivalent to this.

Answer _____

Part B Explain how you know the expressions are equivalent.

_____

_____

_____

17 Venus will evaluate the expression shown below.

$$40 \div 2^3 - 5 + 3 \times 2$$

Part A List all the operations in the order that they should be performed. Be sure to include the exponent.

Answer _____

Part B What is the value of this expression? Show your work.

Answer _____

UNIT 6

Equations and Inequalities

- **Lesson 1 Equations and Inequalities** reviews what an equation and an inequality are and how to tell if given values make them true.

- **Lesson 2 Writing Equations** reviews how to write equations to represent problem situations.

- **Lesson 3 Solving Equations** reviews solving one-step equations including those represented in word problems.

- **Lesson 4 Representing Inequalities** reviews how to find solution sets of inequalities including those on a number line and how to use inequalities to represent real-world situations.

A balenced scale can represent an equation that is true.

The symbol ≠ means "is not equal to."

An **equation** is a mathematical statement that shows two expressions are equal. Some equations have variables. The **solution** of an equation is the value of the variable that makes the equation true.

Which value of n—13 or 17—is a solution to $8 + n = 21$?

Substitute each value for n to see which gives a true equation.

When $n = 13$, $8 + 13 = 21$.   When $n = 17$, $8 + 17 \neq 21$.

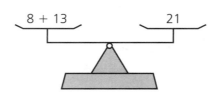
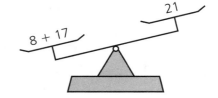

$n = 13$ is a solution. $n = 17$ is not a solution.

The **inequality symbols** are

  < "is less than"

  > "is greater than"

  ≤ "is less than or
    equal to"

  ≥ "is greater than or
    equal to"

Equations typically have only one solution.

Inequalities have more than one solution.

An **inequality** is a mathematical statement that compares two expressions using inequality symbols. Some inequalities have variables. The solutions of an inequality are the values of the variable that makes the inequality true.

Which values of y—4, 16, or 20—are solutions to $y \div 2 > 8$?

Substitute each value for y to see which gives a true inequality.

When $y = 4$, $4 \div 2 < 8$. The inequality $y \div 2 > 8$ is not true for $y = 4$. $y = 4$ is not a solution.

When $y = 16$, $16 \div 2 = 8$. The inequality $y \div 2 > 8$ is not true for $y = 16$. $y = 16$ is not a solution.

When $y = 20$, $20 \div 2 > 8$. The inequality $y \div 2 > 8$ is true for $y = 20$. $y = 20$ is a solution.

SAMPLE Which value of x is **not** a solution to the inequality below?

$$5x \geq 13$$

A 2   **B** 3   **C** 4   **D** 5

The correct answer is A. Substitute each value for x. Find the value that makes the inequality false. When $x = 2$, $5(2) \geq 13$ is false. So 2 is not a solution. Check that the other choices are solutions. When $x = 3$, $5(3) \geq 13$. So 3 is a solution. When $x = 4$, $5(4) \geq 13$. So 4 is a solution. When $x = 5$, $5(5) \geq 13$. So 5 is a solution.

1 Which equation is true?

  A $7 \times 8 = 54$ **C** $50 - 32 = 28$

  B $29 + 49 = 68$ **D** $63 \div 9 = 7$

2 Which value of d makes the scale below balanced?

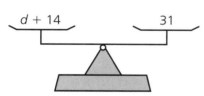

  A 13   **C** 23

  B 17   **D** 27

3 Which inequality is true?

  A $6 \div 2 < 4$ **C** $32 \div 4 < 8$

  B $3 \times 7 > 23$ **D** $9 \times 5 > 46$

4 Which of the following represents an equation?

  A $5 + 12$ **C** $6 + 9 = 15$

  B $3 + x$ **D** $7 + 2 > 6$

5 Mindy is 3 inches taller than Keira. Keira is 60 inches tall. The equation $m - 3 = 60$ can be used to find Mindy's height. Which value of m makes this equation true?

  A 53   **C** 63

  B 57   **D** 67

6 Is 7 a solution to $21 - w \leq 14$?

  A Yes, because the expression on the left can equal the expression on the right.

  B Yes, because the expression on the left is less than the expression on the right.

  C No, because the expression on the left should be less than the expression on the right.

  D No, because the expression on the left should be greater than the expression on the right.

7 For which inequality is $b = 12$ a solution?

  A $3b > 36$ **C** $b + 6 < 16$

  B $b \div 3 > 5$ **D** $15 - b < 5$

SAMPLE Mr. Blake stays in a hotel for 3 nights. The total cost is $234. The equation $3h = 234$ can be used to find h, the cost of one night at the hotel. Does the cost of one night equal $78? Explain how you know.

_____

_____

> ✓ Substitute 78 for h in the equation to see if it is true. $3(78) = 234$ is true, so the cost of one night at the hotel is $78.

8 The expressions $n - 5$ and 33 are equal. Which of these numbers—22, 28, 32, and 38—could be the value of n?

Answer _____

9 Write an equation that has a solution of $x = 8$.

Answer _____

10 Of the numbers 1, 2, 3, 4, and 5, which are solutions to the inequality $7 - k > 4$?

Answer _____

11 Carlos wants to save $25 each week until he has saved at least $400. The inequality $25w \geq 400$ can be used to find the number of weeks it will take Carlos to save that amount of money. Will it take more than 15 weeks or less than 15 weeks for Carlos to save $400? Explain how you know.

_____

_____

_____

12 The scale below is balanced.

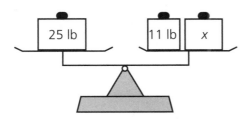

Part A Andrea has 12-lb, 14-lb, and 16-lb weights. Which size weight could represent the weight labeled *x?*

Answer _____

The weights on the scale below cause it to be unbalanced.

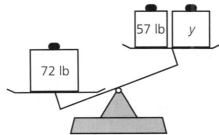

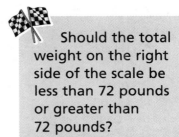

Should the total weight on the right side of the scale be less than 72 pounds or greater than 72 pounds?

Part B Anton has 12-lb, 14-lb, 16-lb, and 18-lb weights. Which sizes could represent the weight labeled *y?* Explain how you know.

_____

_____

_____

Key words used in translating operations are

(+) add
sum
plus
increased by
more than
all together

(−) subtract
difference
minus
fewer
less than
decreased by
take away
how much more

(×) multiply
product
times
groups of
in all

(÷) divide
quotient
groups of
share
split equally

Look for key words to help translate words into an equation. Key words help determine which operation to use.

Write the sentence as an equation.

The product of a number n and 8 is 72.

Look for key words that tell what operation to use. *Product* indicates multiplication. *Is* means "equals." The product of a number n and 8 is 72 translates to $8n = 72$.

Equations are used to model everyday situations. You can use what you know about translating words into expressions to help translate words into equations.

All shoes at a store are discounted $15. Bethany pays $24 for one pair after the discount. Write an equation that can be used to find s, the original price of the shoes.

Discounted $15 means $15 is subtracted from the original price, s. This gives the expression $s - 15$. The amount Bethany pays goes on the other side of the equal sign. The equation is $s - 15 = 24$.

Some word situations translate into two-step equations. **Two-step equations** involve more than one operation.

Lamont had some mints. He ate 3 of them and gave the rest to 2 friends to share equally. Each friend got 5 mints. Write an equation that can be used to find m, the number of mints Lamont originally had.

Ate implies subtraction, so the expression $m - 3$ represents the number of mints left before they were shared. *Share equally* means the mints left are divided by 2. This gives the expression $\frac{m - 3}{2}$. The total each friend got goes on the other side of the equal sign. The equation is $\frac{m - 3}{2} = 5$.

SAMPLE A total of 15 campers go canoeing. Each canoe holds up to 3 people. Which equation can be used to find the fewest number of canoes, *c,* the campers use?

A $3c = 15$

B $15c = 3$

C $3 \div c = 15$

D $c \div 3 = 15$

The correct answer is A. Look for key words. The words *total of 15* can be translated as "= 15." The words *fewest number of canoes* means that each canoe will hold 3 people, not less than that. Multiplication is used to find groups of equal size, so the equation is $3c = 15$.

1 Which equation can be used to show the quotient of 18 and *n* is 2?

A $n \div 18 = 2$

C $n - 18 = 2$

B $18 \div n = 2$

D $18 - n = 2$

2 The difference of 10 and the product of *n* and 2 is 4. Which equation models this?

A $2n - 10 = 4$

C $10 - 2n = 4$

B $2(n - 10) = 4$

D $2(10 - n) = 4$

3 A memory card from a digital camera can hold up to 1,752 pictures. So far 183 pictures are on the memory card. Which equation can be used to find *p,* the number of pictures the memory card can still hold?

A $p - 183 = 1,752$

B $183 - p = 1,752$

C $p + 183 = 1,752$

D $p \div 183 = 1,752$

4 Ben put $200 in a bank account at the beginning of the year. For 6 months, he put *d* dollars more into it monthly. At the end of the 6 months, he had $800 in the account. Which equation can be used to find *d?*

A $200 + 6d = 800$

B $d(200 + 6) = 800$

C $200 \times 6 + d = 800$

D $200 + 6 + d = 800$

5 Morgan had $28 in her wallet. She spent *k* dollars and had $17 left. Morgan wrote the equation $k - 28 = 17$ to help find the value of *k.* Is this equation correct?

A Yes, because 28 is being subtracted.

B No, because 17 and 28 should be switched.

C No, because the variable and 17 should be switched.

D No, because the variable should be subtracted from 28.

SAMPLE Dante earns $20 each hour he works. Last week, $160 was taken out of his earnings for taxes. After taxes were taken out, he received $640. Write an equation that can be used to find h, the number of hours Dante worked last week.

Answer _____

✓ Multiplication is used to relate hourly pay and hours worked. The expression $20h$ represents Dante's earnings before taxes. Subtraction is used to show a decrease from taxes. So, the equation $20h - 160 = 640$ represents this situation.

6 The cost to pick berries at a farm is $2 each pound. Michaela picked p pounds of berries and paid $9. Write an equation that can be used to find p.

Answer _____

7 Leah collects coins. She had 372 coins in her collection. She collected the same number of additional coins during the next 4 weeks. At the end of that time, she had 432 coins. What equation can be used to find c, the number of coins Leah collected each of the 4 weeks?

Answer _____

8 In 4 hours, Max drove 200 miles. Write a multiplication equation and a division equation that can both be used to find the average rate of speed, r, in miles per hour, Max drove.

Answer _____

9 Write a problem that can be solved using the equation $2n \div 3 = 10$.

_____

_____

10 A box contains 15 ounces of cereal. The box has a total of 20 servings.

Part A Write an equation that can be used to find n, the number of ounces per serving of cereal.

Answer _____

Part B Write an equation, using a different operation than the one you used in part A that can be used to find n.

Answer _____

11 The quotient of a number x and 5 less than 75 is 15.

Part A Which operations can you use to write an equation to show this?

Answer _____

Part B Write an equation that can be used to find x. Explain how you know that is the correct equation.

_____

_____

_____

Make sure to put the given numbers and variables in the correct order.

Solving Equations

6.EE.7

To solve equations, undo the operation in the equation. **Inverse operations** undo each other.

Addition and subtraction are inverse operations.

Multiplication and division are inverse operations.

What value of y makes this equation true?

$$y + 8 = 26$$

This is an addition equation. Use subtraction, the inverse operation of addition, to solve.

8 is being added, so subtract 8 from each side.

$$y + 8 - 8 = 26 - 8$$
$$y = 18$$

Sometimes you need to write an equation to model a situation and then solve it.

About 8 million people live in New York City. This is about 4 times as many people as live in Houston, Texas. About how many people live in Houston?

First write an equation to model the situation. Then solve it.

8 million in New York City = 4 × people in Houston
$$8 = 4p$$

The inverse of multiplication is division. Divide both sides of the equation by 4.

$$\frac{8}{4} = \frac{4p}{4}$$

$$p = 2$$

About 2 million people live in Houston, Texas.

Use the inverse operation on *both* sides of the equation to keep it balanced.

Substitute your answer into the original equation to check your work.

$$8 = 4p$$
$$8 = 4(2)$$
$$8 = 8$$

The equation is true, so the answer is correct.

SAMPLE Norman had 53 postcards. He bought some more. Now he has 61 postcards. How many postcards did he buy?

    A 2   **B** 8   **C** 9   **D** 12

The correct answer is B. First, write an equation to model the situation: $x + 53 = 61$. To solve this, subtract 53 from both sides: $x + 53 - 53 = 61 - 53 \rightarrow x = 8$.

1 What operation should be used to solve the equation $25n = 1{,}200$?

  A addition   **C** multiplication

  B subtraction   **D** division

2 Polly wants to solve the equation below.

$$77 = z + 39$$

What should she do to both sides of the equation?

  A add 39   **C** subtract 39

  B add 77   **D** subtract 77

3 In which equation is 14 subtracted from both sides to find the value of k?

  A $k + 4 = 14$ **C** $k + 14 = 42$

  B $k - 4 = 14$ **D** $k - 14 = 42$

4 Which equation shows how to correctly solve $5n = 30$ for n?

  A $5n + 5 = 30 + 5$

  B $5n - 5 = 30 - 5$

  C $5n \times 5 = 30 \times 5$

  D $5n \div 5 = 30 \div 5$

5 Alice will drive a total of 240 miles. So far she has driven 80 miles. How many more miles does Alice need to drive?

  A 3   **C** 320

  B 160   **D** 1,920

6 The area of a rectangle is 50 square feet. The width of the rectangle is 10 feet. What is the length of the rectangle?

  A 5 feet   **C** 60 feet

  B 40 feet   **D** 500 feet

7 What is the solution to the equation $12 = 6w$?

  A $w = 2$ **C** $w = 18$

  B $w = 6$ **D** $w = 72$

8 A car tire is fully inflated when it has 44 pounds of air. A car tire now has 28 pounds of air. How much more air is needed to fully inflate the tire?

  A 2 pounds   **C** 16 pounds

  B 14 pounds   **D** 28 pounds

SAMPLE Laura solved an equation as shown below.

$$b + 6 = 20$$
$$\underline{+6 \quad +6}$$
$$b \quad\quad = 26$$

Is the solution correct? Explain how you know.

_____

_____

No, it is not correct. To solve addition equations, you must use the inverse operation, subtraction. This means 6 should be subtracted from both sides of the equation, not added. So, b should be $20 - 6 = 14$.

9 What is the inverse operation of division?

Answer _____

10 Ethan rented a car for 5 days. He paid a total of $110. What was the average cost per day to rent the car?

Answer _____

11 Vincent wants to solve the equation $z + 484 = 964$. He writes the equation below to find the value of z.

$$z + 484 = 964 - 484$$

Will Vincent get the correct answer using this equation? Explain how you know.

_____

_____

12 This table shows the amount of money some movies made during their opening week at the theater.

MONEY MOVIES MADE OPENING WEEK

Movie	Amount of Money ($)
Charlie's Adventures	310,000
Jackpot	930,000
Splash Down	465,000

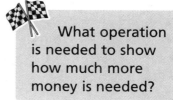

What operation is needed to show how much more money is needed?

Part A How much more money did *Charlie's Adventures* need to make in order to equal the amount of money *Splash Down* made? Write an equation to model this and show how you solved it.

_____

_____

Part B How many times more money did *Jackpot* make than *Charlie's Adventures?* Write an equation to model this and show how you solved it.

_____

_____

Representing Inequalities

6.EE.8

The inequality symbol < means "is less than." The symbol > means "is greater than."

The solution to an inequality is called the **solution set.** A solution set is all the numbers that make an inequality true. A solution set for an inequality has an **infinite,** or countless, number of solutions.

Jorge added $10 to his savings today. Now he has more than $100 in his savings. Write and solve an inequality to show how much Jorge had in his savings before today.

Look for key words to help you write the inequality.

amount in savings before + $10 is more than $100

$$x + 10 > 100$$

Solve inequalities the same way you solve equations. Use inverse operations.

To solve, use inverse operations. Subtract 10 from both sides.

$$x + 10 - 10 > 100 - 10$$

$$x > 90$$

The solution set for the inequality $x > 90$ is all numbers greater than 90.

$x > 90$ is the solution set. Jorge had more than $90 in his savings before today.

A solution set can be graphed on a number line.

Graph the solution set for the example above on a number line.

An open dot on a number line means the number is **not** part of the solution. Open dots are used for inequalities with < and >.

Draw and label a number line with numbers above and below 90. Place an open dot at the number in the solution, 90. Draw an arrow from the dot to the right to show the solution set includes numbers greater than 90.

A closed dot means the number **is** part of the solution. Closed dots are used for inequalities with ≤ or ≥.

UNIT 6 ▓▓
Equations and Inequalities

SAMPLE A bicycle costs less than $300. The bicycle costs 5 times more than a skateboard. Which inequality shows the cost, in dollars, of the skateboard?

    A $s < 60$ **B** $s > 60$ **C** $s < 1{,}500$ **D** $s > 1{,}500$

> The correct answer is A. First, write an inequality to model the situation. Let s represent the cost of the skateboard: $5s < 300$. To solve this inequality, divide both sides by 5: $5s \div 5 < 300 \div 5$. This gives $s < 60$.

1 Which number line shows the solution set for $x > 22$?

A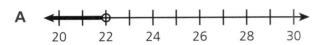

B

C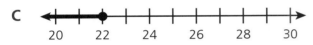

D

2 An office building has fewer than 13 floors. Which inequality best models this?

    A $f < 13$ **C** $f \le 13$

    B $f > 13$ **D** $f \ge 13$

3 How many solutions are there in the solution set of $2x < 6$?

    A 1   **C** 12

    B 3   **D** infinitely many

4 Logan is 4 times older than his cousin Dylan. Logan is less than 12 years old. Which inequality shows the possible age Dylan could be?

    A $d < 3$ **C** $d < 48$

    B $d > 3$ **D** $d > 48$

5 Julia made the number line below to shows the solution set of the inequality $x + 8 > 10$.

Is this number line correct?

A Yes, the solution set includes all numbers greater than or equal to 2.

B No, the solution set does not include the number 2.

C No, the solution set should include all numbers less than 2.

D No, the solution set should include all numbers greater than 18.

SAMPLE Alaska has a land area of more than 500,000 square miles. The land area of Delaware is 250 times less than this. Write an inequality to represent the land area, in square miles, of Delaware.

Answer _____

Let d represent the land area of Delaware. The key word *times* indicates multiplication. The key words *is less than* indicate $<$. So, $250d < 500,000$. To solve this inequality, divide both sides by 250: $250d \div 250 < 500,000 \div 250$. This gives $d < 2,000$.

6 In the space below, draw a number line to show the solution set for x is less than 5.

7 The sum of 31 and k is greater than 85. What is the solution set for k?

Answer _____

8 An airline can sell less than 155 tickets for a flight. So far 97 tickets have been sold. Denzel made the number line below to show the number of tickets the airline is still able to sell.

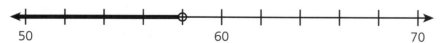

Is this number line correct? Explain how you know.

_____

_____

_____

UNIT 6 ▩▩▩▩▩▩▩▩▩▩▩▩▩▩▩▩▩▩▩▩▩▩▩▩▩▩▩▩▩▩▩▩▩▩▩
Equations and Inequalities

9 Rachel drew this number line to model the solution set for an inequality.

Part A What inequality is modeled by this number line?

Answer _____

Rachel delivers newspapers. She earns the same dollar amount each week. In 8 weeks, she earned more than $600.

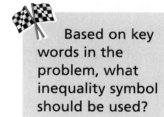
Based on key words in the problem, what inequality symbol should be used?

Part B Does the number line above represent the amount of money Rachel earns delivering newspapers each week? Explain how you know.

_____

_____

10 Uma scored 3 more points than Hanna. Hanna scored more than 30 points.

Part A Write an inequality to represent the number of points, *p,* Uma scored.

Answer _____

Part B In the space below, draw a number line to show the solution set to the inequality you wrote.

REVIEW

Equations and Inequalities

Read each problem. Circle the letter of the best answer.

1 Beth wants to solve the equation $4z = 52$. What should she do to both sides of the equation?

   A add 4   **C** multiply by 4

   B subtract 4   **D** divide by 4

2 The quotient of 20 and t is 10. Which equation models this?

   A $\frac{t}{20} = 10$ **C** $20 \times t = 10$

   B $\frac{20}{t} = 10$ **D** $20 - t = 10$

3 School vacation starts in less than 4 weeks. Which inequality best models this?

   A $v < 4$ **C** $v \leq 4$

   B $v > 4$ **D** $v \geq 4$

4 Which value of m makes the scale below balanced?

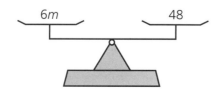

   A 6   **C** 42

   B 8   **D** 54

5 Which inequality is true?

   A $10 + 3 < 13$ **C** $21 - 9 < 14$

   B $11 + 11 > 23$ **D** $30 - 16 > 15$

6 A photocopier can make 20 copies per minute. Which equation can be used to find m, the number of minutes the copier takes to make 75 copies?

   A $20m = 75$ **C** $m \div 20 = 75$

   B $75m = 20$ **D** $20 \div m = 75$

7 Hugo rents a mailbox that costs 2 times more than the mailbox Andrey rents. The cost of the mailbox Andrey rents is more than $40 a year. Which number line shows the possible cost, in dollars per year, of the mailbox Hugo rents?

A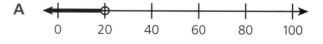

B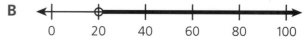

C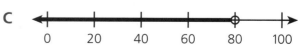

D

8 What operation should be used to solve the equation below?

$$25h = 325$$

Answer _____

9 Of the numbers 1, 2, 3, 4, and 5, which are solutions to the inequality $n + 6 > 9$?

Answer _____

10 A number less than 24 is 7. Write an equation that can be used to find the number.

Answer _____

11 Pilar bought a box of nails and a hammer. The hammer cost $12. All together, Pilar spent more than $15. Write an inequality to find the possible cost of the box of nails and draw a number line to graph its solution set.

Answer _____

12 Coral wants to solve the equation $200y = 50$. She writes the equation below to find the value of y.

$$200y \div 50 = 50 \div 50$$

Will Coral get the correct answer using this equation? Explain how you know.

_____

_____

13 A total of 210 charms are put into 7 boxes. Each box has the same number of charms.

 Part A Write an equation that can be used to find c, the number of charms in each box.

 Answer _____

 Part B Write another equation, using a different operation than the one you used in part A, which can be used to find c.

 Answer _____

14 Aiden drew this number line to model the solution set for an inequality.

 Part A What inequality is modeled by this number line?

 Answer _____

A truck has a gas tank that holds 22 gallon of gas. The truck travels less than 330 miles on one tank of gas.

 Part B Does the number line above represent the average number of miles the truck can travel on one gallon of gas? Explain how you know.

_____

_____

_____

Relationships Between Two Variables

● **Lesson 1 Functions** reviews how to find the relationship between two variables in equations and in tables.

● **Lesson 2 Graphing Relationships** reviews how to graph the relationship between two variables on a coordinate plane.

:: **UNIT 7**
Relationships Between Two Variables

123

Functions

6.EE.9

A **function** shows the relationship between values from one set of numbers to another set. The first set of numbers is the **input.** The second set of numbers is the **output.**

Equations can be written to represent a function. Two variables are used in functions. One represents the input. The other represents the output.

> Hoshi's school club washes cars to earn money. They earn $5 for each car they wash. Write an equation to represent the amount of money the club can earn.

> Find the relationship, or rule, that exists in this problem. The problem says they earn $5 for each car washed. The rule is "multiply by 5."

> Define the input and the output. The input is the number of cars washed. The output is the total amount of money earned.

$$5 \times \text{input} = \text{output}$$

> Let x represent the input and y represent the output. The equation is $5x = y$.

Function tables can also be used to represent a function.

> Make a function table to show the amount of money Hoshi's school club earns washing 5, 10, 15, and 20 cars.

> The rule is "multiply by 5." The input values are 5, 10, 15, and 20. Apply the rule to the input values to find the output values.

Input	Output
5	25
10	50
15	75
20	100

> Each output is 5 times the corresponding input.

The variable x is often used to represent the input. This is also called the **independent variable.**

The variable y is often used to represent the output. This is also called the **dependent variable.**

Tables used to represent functions are sometimes called **input-output tables.**

If you know the rule and the output value, you can find the input by using the inverse operation.

SAMPLE A function rule is "add 7." The output value is 22. What is the input value?

A 15 B 17 C 27 D 29

The correct answer is A. You are given the rule and the output. To find the input, use the inverse operation of the rule. The inverse of "add 7" is "subtract 7." So, subtract 7 from 22 to find the input: $22 - 7 = 15$.

1 A function rule is "divide by 4." What is the output when the input is 100?

A 25 C 50

B 40 D 400

2 What is the rule for this input-output table?

Input	Output
10	5
20	15
30	25
40	35

A add 10 C multiply by 2

B subtract 5 D divide by 2

3 What is the missing number in this input-output table?

Input	Output
8	24
10	30
16	48
?	63

A 18 C 21

B 19 D 23

4 When the input is 8, the output is 2. When the input is 12, the output is 3. Which equation could model the rule used to change the input to the output?

A output = input + 6

B output = input − 6

C output = input × 4

D output = input ÷ 4

5 A function is shown in this input-output table.

x	y
1	9
3	11
5	13
7	15

Which statement describes the relationship between x and y?

A y is 2 times x.

B y is 9 times x.

C y is 2 more than x.

D y is 8 more than x.

SAMPLE A function machine is shown below.

Input   Output

6 → _____ → 18

9 → _____ → 27

What is the output from this function machine when the input is 13?

Answer _____

First find the rule that changes each input to the given output. To change 6 to 18, either add 12 or multiply by 3. To change 9 to 27, either add 18 or multiply by 3. The rule these inputs have in common is "multiply by 3." So, when the input is 13, the output is 3 × 13 = 39.

6 What is the rule shown in this table?

x	y
0	0
8	1
16	2

Answer _____

7 A deluxe hotel room costs $20 more than a standard hotel room. The function $y = x + 20$ shows the relationship between the cost of a standard hotel room, x, and the cost of a deluxe hotel room, y. What is the value of x when y is $150?

Answer _____

UNIT 7 :::
Relationships Between Two Variables

8 This table shows the relationship between the weight of a salad at a salad bar and the cost of the salad.

SALAD BAR

Weight (ounces)	Cost ($)
4	1
8	2
12	3
16	4

Look for a common relationship between each row in the table.

Part A Describe in words the relationship between the weight of the salad and the cost of the salad at this salad bar.

_____

_____

Part B Fred buys a salad for his family at this salad bar. He pays $9 for the salad. What is the weight, in ounces, of Fred's salad? Explain how you know.

_____

_____

_____

9 Sue is 6 years older than Jenny. Let x represent Sue's age. Let y represent Jenny's age.

Part A What equation shows the relationship between x and y?

Answer _____

Part B If Jenny is 19 years old, how old is Sue?

Answer _____

Graphing Relationships

6.EE.9

The horizontal axis on a coordinate plane is the x-axis. The vertical axis is the y-axis.

The x-coordinate of a point tells how many places to move along the x-axis. The y-coordinate tells how many places to move up or down from the x-coordinate.

The points on a linear function can have positive and negative coordinates.

In some situations, it does not make sense to have negative values for x or y. In these cases, the graphs should appear in quadrant I only.

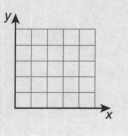

A **linear function** is a function represented by a straight line. Each input in a linear function has exactly one output. Linear functions can be graphed on a coordinate plane.

Graph the function $y = 3x$ on a coordinate plane.

First make an input-output table for this function. Choose any values for x and find the corresponding y-values.

x	y
0	0
1	3
2	6
3	9

The values in the table can be written as the ordered pairs (0, 0), (1, 3), (2, 6), and (3, 9).

Draw a coordinate plane. Graph each point from the table on the plane. Then connect the points with a straight line, in each direction.

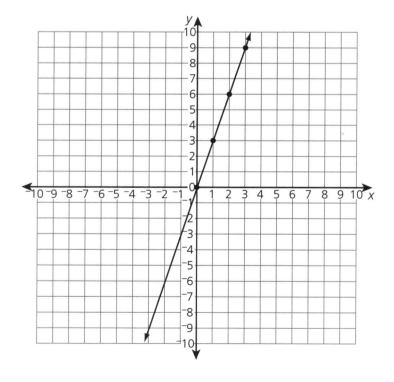

SAMPLE What is the *y*-coordinate for the point where *x* = –3 on the graph of this linear function?

A –1 C –3

B –2 D –4

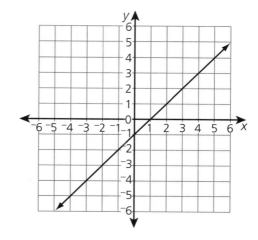

   The correct answer is D. First start at the origin (0, 0) and move left along the *x*-axis 3 units. This is the point *x* = –3. From here, move down until you reach the line. Look directly to the right to find the *y*-value that lines up with the graph. The *y*-coordinate is –4.

1 This graph shows the relationship between the time, in hours, a car travels and the distance, in miles, it travels.

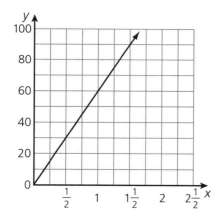

Which point is on this line?

A (1, 20) C (1, 60)

B (1, 40) D (1, 100)

2 A function is shown in this input-output table.

x	–1	0	1	2
y	–2	0	2	4

It has been graphed on the plane below.

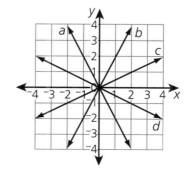

Which graph shows the relationship between *x* and *y*?

A line *a* C line *c*

B line *b* D line *d*

SAMPLE A function follows the rule that y is 5 less than x. Name two different points that are on the graph of this function.

Answer _____

First write an equation to represent this function rule: "y is 5 less than x" translates to $y = x - 5$. Next, pick any two values for x and find the y-values that correspond. If $x = 10$, $y = 10 - 5 = 5$. If $x = 11$, $y = 11 - 5 = 6$. So two points on the graph are (10, 5) and (11, 6).

3 On the coordinate plane below, draw the graph of the function $y = x - 2$.

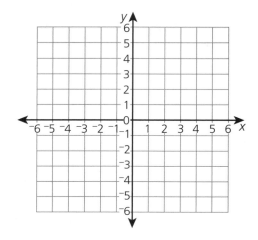

4 This graph shows the relationship between the number of hours Eli works, x, and the amount of money he earns, y.

Explain how the amount of money Eli earns changes as the number of hours he works increases.

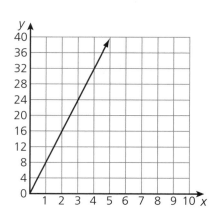

_____

_____

_____

_____

5 Alea made the function table below.

x	y
3	18
5	30
8	48
10	60

Part A Describe in words the relationship between *x* and *y*.
Then write an equation to model this function.

_____

_____

Part B On the coordinate plane below, draw the line
represented by this function.

Be sure to label each axis with appropriate numbers based on the numbers in the table.

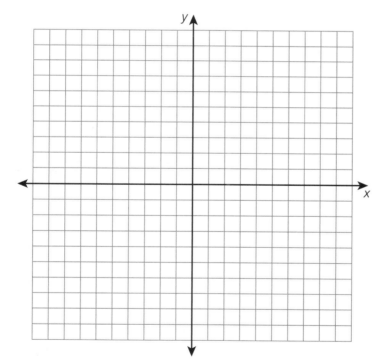

REVIEW

Relationships Between Two Variables

Read each problem. Circle the letter of the best answer.

1 A function rule is "subtract 8." What is the output when the input is 41?

  A 33   **C** 47

  B 37   **D** 49

2 What is the rule for this input-output table?

Input	Output
6	2
18	6
24	8

  A add 4   **C** multiply by 3

  B subtract 4   **D** divide by 3

3 Which line shows the function $y = x + 4$?

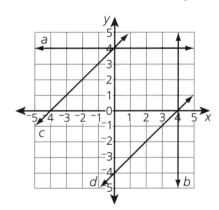

  A line *a*   **C** line *c*

  B line *b*   **D** line *d*

4 Nadia buys a sandwich at the deli. This graph shows the relationship between the dollar amount she could give the clerk, *x*, and the dollar amount of change she could receive back, *y*.

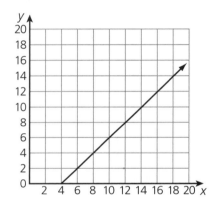

Which point is on this graph?

  A (8, 6)   **C** (12, 12)

  B (10, 14)   **D** (14, 10)

5 A bus ticket costs $2.50 less than a train ticket. Let *x* be the cost of the bus ticket. Let *y* be the cost of the train ticket. Which equation show the relationship of *x* to *y*?

  A $y = x + 2.5$ **C** $y = 2.5x$

  B $y = x - 2.5$ **D** $y = 2.5 - x$

6 A function follows the rule that y is 12 more than x. Name two different points that are on the graph of this function.

Answer _____

7 A function machine is shown below.

Input		Output
14 →		→ 7
21 →		→ 14

What is the output from this function machine when the input is 42?

Answer _____

8 There are 45 fewer sixth graders than seventh graders in Armand's school. The function $y = x + 45$ shows the relationship between the number of sixth graders, x, and the number of seventh graders, y. What is the value of x when y is 210?

Answer _____

9 Drew has a bank loan. He pays money towards the loan each month. This table shows the relationship between the number of months Drew made payments toward the loan and the dollar amount left on it.

LOAN PAYMENTS

Number of Payments	Amount Left on Loan ($)
1	2,000
2	1,850
3	1,700
4	1,550

Explain how the amount left to pay on the loan changes as the number of payments increases.

_____

_____

10 Erin wrote the function $y = x + 50$.

Part A Make an x–y table of values to model this function for
x-values 0, 10, 20, and 30.

x	y

Part B Graph this function on the coordinate plane below. Be sure
to label each axis with appropriate values.

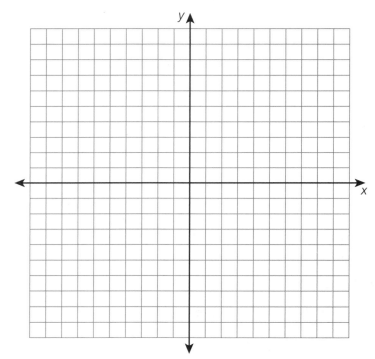

Geometry

- **Lesson 1 Area** reviews how to find the area of different geometric figures and how to use area to solve problems.

- **Lesson 2 Volume** reviews how to find the volume of rectangular prisms.

- **Lesson 3 Nets and Surface Area** reviews what nets are and how to use them to find the surface area of three-dimensional figures.

- **Lesson 4 Coordinate Geometry** reviews how to draw polygons and find lengths of the sides of the polygons on a coordinate plane.

Area

6.G.1

The **area** of a figure is the number of square units inside the figure. To find area, you can either count the number of square units inside the figure or you can use **area formulas.**

Square units are units that are squared, or raised to the 2nd power. Some examples of square units include

square inches = in.²
square feet = ft²
square meters = m²

To find the area of this

figure, , count the number of squares inside it. There are 8 squares inside, so the area is 8 square units.

Area of a **triangle**

$\frac{1}{2}bh = \frac{1}{2}$ base × height

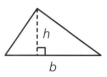

Area of a **rectangle**

lw = length × width

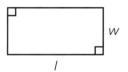

Area of a **parallelogram**

bh = base × height

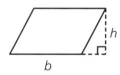

Area of a **trapezoid**

$\frac{1}{2}(b_1 + b_2)h =$
$\frac{1}{2}$(base₁ + base₂)height

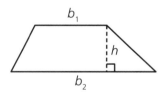

You can also find the area of the patio by dividing the figure into a rectangle and a triangle.

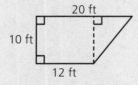

Find the areas of each separate figure and add them together.

The shape of Joy's patio is shown in this diagram.

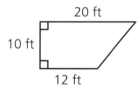

What is the area of the patio?

The patio is a trapezoid. To find its area, use the formula $\frac{1}{2}(b_1 + b_2)h$ and the values $b_1 = 20$ ft, $b_2 = 12$ ft, and $h = 10$ ft.

$$\frac{1}{2}(b_1 + b_2)h = \frac{1}{2}(20 + 12)10 = \frac{1}{2}(32)(10) = 160$$

The area of the patio is 160 square feet.

SAMPLE This diagram shows the back of a birdhouse. What is the area of the back side of the birdhouse?

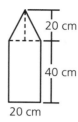

    A   800 cm²   **C**   1,200 cm²

    B   1,000 cm²   **D**   1,600 cm²

The correct answer is B. This diagram can be divided into a triangle and a rectangle. Find the area of each of these shapes and then add them together. The base and the height of the triangle are both 20 cm. So its area is $\frac{1}{2}(20)(20) = 200$ cm². The length and width of the rectangle are 20 cm and 40 cm, so its area is $20(40) = 800$ cm². The total area is $200 + 800 = 1,000$ cm².

1 A computer screen has a length of 16 inches and a width of 12 inches. What is the area of the computer screen?

    A   96 in.   **C**   192 in.

    B   96 in.²   **D**   192 in.²

2 What is the area, in square units, of the figure below?

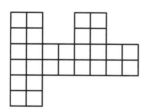

    A   20 units²   **C**   28 units²

    B   24 units²   **D**   32 units²

3 The bases of a trapezoid are 10 cm and 15 cm. The height of the trapezoid is 8 cm. What is the area of the trapezoid?

    A   100 cm²   **C**   600 cm²

    B   200 cm²   **D**   1,200 cm²

4 What is the area of this parallelogram?

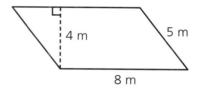

    A   20 m²   **C**   40 m²

    B   32 m²   **D**   160 m²

5 New carpet will be put in the room shown in the diagram below.

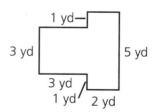

What is the area of the room?

    A   15 yd²   **C**   19 yd²

    B   18 yd²   **D**   25 yd²

SAMPLE The height of a triangle is 3 times its base. The base of the triangle is 6 inches. What is the area, in square inches, of the triangle?

Answer _____

First find the base and the height of the triangle. Then use the formula to find the area of a triangle. It is given that the base is 6 inches and the height is 3 times the base. So, the height is $6 \times 3 = 18$ in. The formula for the area of a triangle is $\frac{1}{2}bh = \frac{1}{2}(6)(18) = 54$. The area is 54 in.^{2}.

6 What is the area, in square units, of the shape at the right?

Answer _____

7 What is the area of the triangular sign shown at the right? Show your work.

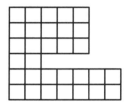

30 in.

SLOW

30 in.

Answer _____

8 Andy thinks the area of this parallelogram is 24 ft^2. Is he correct? Explain how you know.

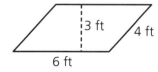

3 ft

4 ft

6 ft

_____

_____

9 Chantal cut a piece of fabric for a banner in the shape shown below.

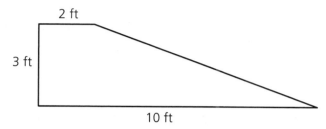

Part A What is the area of the banner? Show your work.

What are the height and base lengths of this figure?

Answer _____

Part B Explain how you could use exactly one formula and how you could use more than one formula to find the area of this banner.

_____

_____

_____

_____

Volume

6.G.2

Cubic units are units that are cubed, or raised to the 3rd power. Some examples of cubic units include

cubic inches = in.^{3}
cubic feet = ft^3
cubic meters = m^3

A **unit cube** is a cube with a side length of 1 unit and has a volume of 1 cubic unit.

1 in.

The volume of this 1-inch cube is 1 cubic inch.

The volume of a rectangular prism also equals the product of the area of its base and its height.

V = (area of base) × height

A **three-dimensional figure** is a solid figure with length, width, and height. The amount of space inside a three-dimensional figure is called **volume.** Volume is measured in **cubic units.**

How many unit cubes does it take to fill the box below?

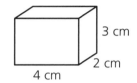

Fill the box with unit cubes that have a volume of 1 cm^3 each. The base, or bottom, fits 8 unit cubes.

Since the box is 3 cm high, 3 layers of 8 unit cubes fit inside. 3 × 8 = 24 unit cubes fill the box.

A **rectangular prism** is a solid figure with all rectangular sides. The formula for the volume of a rectangular prism is V = length × width × height or $V = lwh$.

A storage box is in the shape of a rectangular prism.

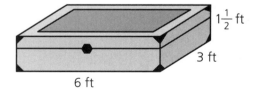

What is the volume of this storage box?

Multiply the length, width, and height of the box.

$$V = lwh = 6 \text{ ft} \times 3 \text{ ft} \times 1\tfrac{1}{2} \text{ ft} = 27$$

The volume is 27 ft^3.

Read each problem. Circle the letter of the best answer.

SAMPLE A tissue box is $3\frac{3}{4}$ inches tall. The area of the base of the tissue box is 60 square inches. What is the volume inside the tissue box?

    A $63\frac{3}{4}$ in.³   **B** $180\frac{3}{4}$ in.³   **C** 200 in.³   **D** 225 in.³

> The correct answer is D. The area of the base of the tissue box is given as 60 square inches. To find the volume of the box, use the formula $V = bh$: $V = 60$ in.² $\times 3\frac{3}{4}$ in. $= 225$ in.³. Choice A is incorrect because the given numbers are added instead of multiplied. Choices B and C are incorrect because the two numbers were multiplied incorrectly.

1 How many unit cubes fit inside the base of this rectangular prism?

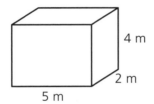

4 m
2 m
5 m

  A 5   **C** 10

  B 7   **D** 20

2 Which expression can be used to find the volume of the box shown below?

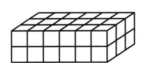

  A 6×2 **C** $6 \times 3 \times 1$

  B 6×3 **D** $6 \times 3 \times 2$

3 What is the volume of the cabinet shown below?

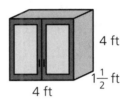

4 ft
$1\frac{1}{2}$ ft
4 ft

  A 24 ft²   **C** 24 ft³

  B 32 ft²   **D** 32 ft³

4 Each side of a cube is 7 centimeters long. What is the volume of this cube?

  A 21 cm³   **C** 147 cm³

  B 49 cm³   **D** 343 cm³

5 A box is filled with 50 cubes. The cubes measure 10 millimeters on each side. What is the volume of the box?

  A 500 mm³   **C** 50,000 mm³

  B 5,000 mm³   **D** 500,000 mm³

SAMPLE The box of pasta shown here is partially filled.

What is the volume, in cubic centimeters, of the pasta inside the box?

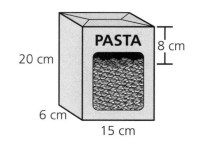

Answer _____

 Only part of the box has pasta. To find the volume of pasta, first find the full volume of the box. Then subtract the volume that has no pasta. Full volume = lwh = 15 × 6 × 20 = 1,800 cm³. The volume of the box without pasta = 15 × 6 × 8 = 720 cm³. The volume of pasta = 1,800 − 720 = 1,080 cm³.

6 The base of a gift box is in the shape of a square. Each side of the base is 6 inches long. The height of the gift box is $4\frac{1}{2}$ inches. Write an expression that can be used to find the volume, in cubic inches, of this gift box.

Answer _____

7 What is the volume, in cubic yards, of the rectangular prism below? Show your work.

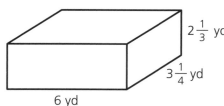

Answer _____

8 José and Ricardo rent a storage unit that is 10 feet wide, 6 feet long, and 8 feet high.

Part A What is the volume, in cubic feet, of the storage unit? Show your work.

Answer _____

Part B José finds the volume of the storage unit by multiplying the length, width, and height. Ricardo finds its volume by multiplying the area of the base by the height. If they both multiply correctly, will the volumes be the same or different? Explain how you know.

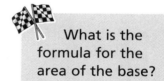

What is the formula for the area of the base?

_____

_____

_____

9 The tank shown below is filled halfway with water.

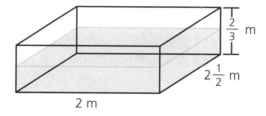

$\frac{2}{3}$ m

$2\frac{1}{2}$ m

2 m

Part A What is the volume, in cubic meters, of the water inside the tank?

Answer _____

Part B Explain how you found your answer.

_____

_____

_____

Nets and Surface Area

6.G.4

 There can be more than one net for the same three-dimensional figure.

A **net** is a two-dimensional representation of a three-dimensional object. A net is formed by unfolding the three-dimensional object.

Draw a net of this rectangular prism.

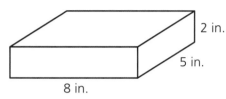

This prism has 6 sides. Imagine unfolding the prism to form a flat two-dimensional figure made up of 6 rectangles. This is its net.

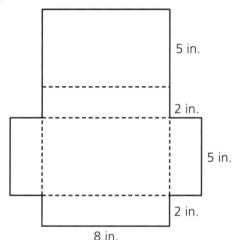

The formula for the surface area of a rectangular prism is $SA = 2lw + 2lh + 2wh$ or $SA = 2(lw + lh + wh)$.

Surface area is measured in square units.

The area of a square is $A = s^2$.

The area of a rectangle is $A = lw$.

The area of a triangle is $A = \frac{1}{2}bh$.

The **surface area** of a three-dimensional object is the sum of the areas of each side of the object. The surface area of a three-dimensional object is equal to the area of its net.

What is the surface area of the rectangular prism above?

From the net, you can see the prism is made up of

- two 8 in. by 5 in. rectangles,
- two 8 in. by 2 in. rectangles, and
- two 2 in. by 5 in. rectangles.

Find the sum of the areas of all of these rectangles.

- 2×8 in. $\times 5$ in. $= 80$ in.^{2}
- 2×8 in. $\times 2$ in. $= 32$ in.^{2}
- 2×2 in. $\times 5$ in. $= 20$ in.^{2}

$$80 \text{ in.}^2 + 32 \text{ in.}^2 + 20 \text{ in.}^2 = 132 \text{ in.}^2$$

The surface area of the rectangular prism is 132 in.^{2}.

SAMPLE What is the surface area of the three-dimensional object formed by this net?

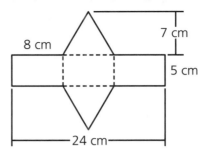

8 cm   7 cm   5 cm   24 cm

A   120 cm²   C   176 cm²

B   131 cm²   D   232 cm²

 The correct answer is C. To find the surface area, sum the areas of the three rectangles and two triangles that make up the net. The area of the rectangles is 3 × 8 cm × 5 cm = 120 cm². The area of the triangles is 2 × ($\frac{1}{2}$ × 8 cm × 7 cm) = 56 cm². The surface area of the object is 120 cm² + 56 cm² = 176 cm².

1 Which two-dimensional figures make up the net of this three-dimensional object?

A   2 squares and 4 rectangles

B   2 rectangles and 4 squares

C   2 triangles and 4 rectangles

D   2 rectangles and 4 triangles

2 Which of the following nets can be folded to form a cube?

A   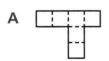   C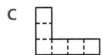

B   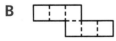   D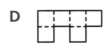

3 A tent with a square-shaped base folds down to the shape represented below.

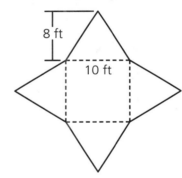

8 ft   10 ft

What is the surface area of the tent?

A   80 ft²   C   260 ft²

B   160 ft²   D   420 ft²

4 A wooden board in the shape of a rectangular prism has a length of 60 inches, a width of 4 inches, and a height of 2 inches. What is the surface area of this wooden board?

A   368 in.²   C   736 in.²

B   480 in.²   D   960 in.²

SAMPLE A toy chest will be assembled. The diagram below shows a net of the unassembled chest.

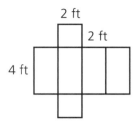

Gwen plans to apply a wood protector on all sides of the toy chest. One can of wood protector covers an area of 15 square feet. How many whole cans of wood protector will Gwen need to buy to cover this entire toy chest?

Answer _____

First find the area of the net. This equals the surface area of the toy chest. The net has four 4-ft by 2-ft sides and two 2-ft by 2-ft sides. The area is $4 \times (4 \text{ ft} \times 2 \text{ ft}) + 2 \times (2 \text{ ft} \times 2 \text{ ft}) = 40 \text{ ft}^2$. Divide this total area by 15 ft^2 and round up to the next whole number to find the number of full cans needed: $40 \text{ ft}^2 \div 15 \text{ ft}^2 = 2\frac{2}{3}$, which rounds up to 3 full cans.

5 Charlotte thinks the surface area of the jewelry box below is 54 in.^{2}.

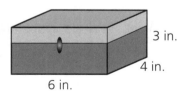

3 in.

4 in.

6 in.

Is this the correct surface area? Explain how you know.

_____

_____

6 Wayne built this ramp out of wood.

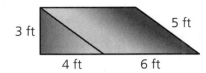

He used two triangles and three rectangles to form the sides of the ramp.

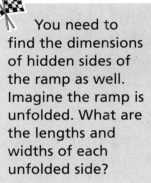

You need to find the dimensions of hidden sides of the ramp as well. Imagine the ramp is unfolded. What are the lengths and widths of each unfolded side?

Part A What are the dimensions of each triangle and rectangle that form the sides of the ramp?

_____

_____

_____

Part B What is the surface area, in square feet, of the ramp? Explain how you know.

_____

_____

_____

7 A photo box is shown below. A picture can be inserted on each face.

4 in.

4 in.

6 in.

Part A What are the shapes and their dimensions that make up the net of this box?

_____

_____

Part B What is the surface area of the photo box?

Answer _____

Coordinate Geometry

6.G.3, 6.NS.8

The plural of *vertex* is *vertices.*

The first number in an ordered pair tells you how far to move left or right from the origin, or center. The second number tells you how far to move up or down from the first number.

For the ordered pair (-2, 4), move left 2 places from the origin. Then move up 4 places from there.

You can find horizontal and vertical side lengths of polygons by counting the number of units from one point to the other.

A **polygon** is a plane geometric figure with straight sides. To draw polygons on a coordinate plane, first graph the points that represent each **vertex,** or corner, of the polygon. Then connect the points with straight lines.

Triangle *ABC* has the points *A* (-2, 4), *B* (4, 6), and *C* (4, 1). Draw triangle *ABC* on a coordinate plane.

Graph vertices *A*, *B*, and *C*. Start at the origin for each point.
For vertex *A*, move left 2 and up 4. Label this point *A*.
For vertex *B*, move right 4 and up 6. Label this point *B*.
For vertex *C*, move right 4 and up 1. Label this point *C*.
Then connect the points with straight lines.

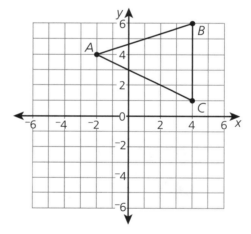

You can find the lengths of horizontal and vertical sides of polygons on a coordinate plane by counting or subtracting coordinates of ordered pairs.

What is the length of side *BC* in the triangle above?

The ordered pairs for points *B* and *C* are (4, 6) and (4, 1). Since the *x*-coordinates are the same, subtract the *y*-coordinates to find the side length.

$$6 - 1 = 5$$

Side *BC* is 5 units long.

Read each problem. Circle the letter of the best answer.

SAMPLE What is the length of side *JK* on this rectangle?

A 3   C 7

B 4   D 8

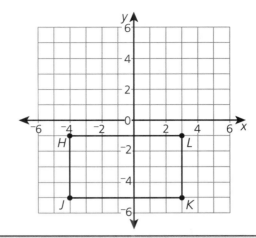

 The correct answer is C. To find the length, count the number of units from point *J* to point *K*. There are 4 units from point *J* to the *y*-axis and 3 units from the *y*-axis to point *K*. All together there are 4 + 3 = 7 units from points *J* to *K*.

1 Polygon *CDEF* is shown on this coordinate plane.

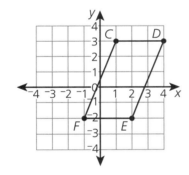

Which expression represents the length of side *CD*?

A 1 − 4   C 4 − 1

B 3 − 3   D 4 − 3

2 A polygon has the coordinates *Q* (-5, 3), *R* (1, 3), *S* (1, -4), and *T*(-5, -2). What name best describes this polygon?

A square   C rectangle

B trapezoid   D parallelogram

3 Which side of this polygon has a length of 6 units?

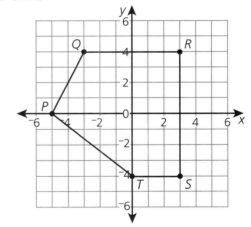

A *QR*   C *ST*

B *RS*   D *TP*

4 One side of a triangle has coordinates at points (-3, 7) and (6, 7). What is the length of this side?

A 3   C 9

B 7   D 14

SAMPLE Polygon *FGHJ* is shown on this coordinate plane.

What is the perimeter, in units, of *FGHJ*?

Answer _____

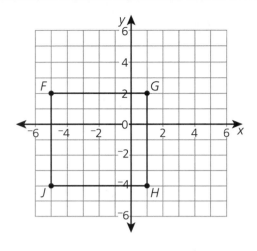

 Count the number of units between each pair of points to find the sides lengths of the polygon. Each side is 6 units long. So, the perimeter of *FGHJ* is 6 + 6 + 6 + 6 = 24 units.

5 Draw and label the triangle with vertices *M* (7, 3), *N* (5, –6), and *P* (-8, –6) on the coordinate plane below.

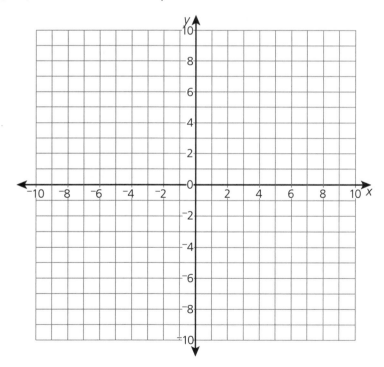

6 Use this coordinate plane to help answer the question.

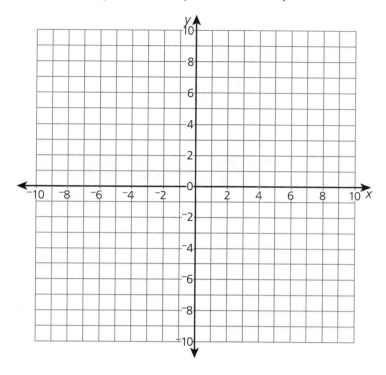

Part A Draw and label the rectangle with vertices *R* (-8, 4), *S* (-8, 0), *T* (5, 0), and *V* (5, 4) on this coordinate plane.

Part B What is the area, in square units, of the rectangle? Explain how you know.

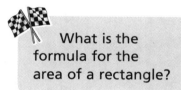

What is the formula for the area of a rectangle?

_____

_____

_____

REVIEW

Geometry

Read each problem. Circle the letter of the best answer.

1 A triangle has a base length of 16 inches and a height of 5 inches. What is its area?

   A 40 in.   **C** 40 in.^{2}

   B 80 in.   **D** 80 in.^{2}

2 A cube-shaped gift box has side lengths of 8 inches each. What is its surface area?

   A 64 in.^{2} **C** 384 in.^{2}

   B 256 in.^{2} **D** 512 in.^{2}

3 What is the area of the trapezoid below?

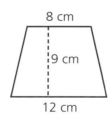

   A 72 cm^2 **C** 108 cm^2

   B 90 cm^2 **D** 432 cm^2

4 A set of 20 toy blocks is packed in a box. Each block measures 3 inches on each side. What is the total volume of the blocks?

   A 60 in.^{3} **C** 360 in.^{3}

   B 180 in.^{3} **D** 540 in.^{3}

5 A donation bin for clothing is shown in the diagram below.

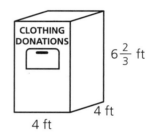

What is the volume of the donation bin?

   A $48\frac{2}{3}$ ft^2 **C** $106\frac{2}{3}$ ft^3

   B $96\frac{2}{3}$ ft^2 **D** $118\frac{2}{3}$ ft^3

6 The net for a box of crackers is represented below.

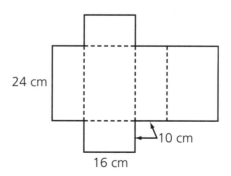

What is the surface area of the box?

   A 384 cm^2 **C** 1,248 cm^2

   B 768 cm^2 **D** 1,568 cm^2

7 The net here represents the shape of a food storage box. What is the surface area, in square inches, of this box?

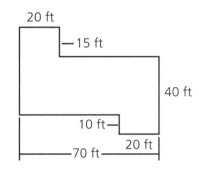

Answer _____

8 The footprint of a house is shown in this diagram. What is the area, in square feet, of the house?

Answer _____

9 Draw and label the polygon with vertices *E* (-4, 0), *F* (7, 0), *G* (7, -7), and *H* (-4, -7) on the coordinate plane below.

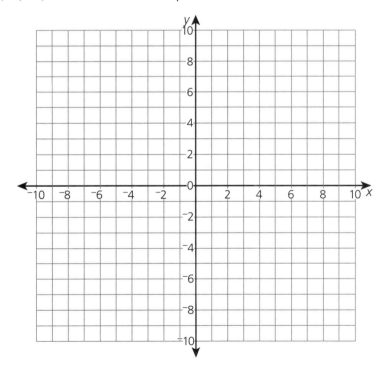

10 Handy Movers sells moving boxes. The base of their large box has an area of 5 square feet. The height of the moving box is $1\frac{1}{2}$ feet.

Part A What is the volume, in cubic feet, of the moving box?

Answer _____

Quality Movers sells a large moving box with the same volume, but different dimensions, as the large box sold by Handy Movers.

Part B What could be the length, width, and height of the large moving box sold by Quality Movers?

Answer _____

11 Rectangle *QRST* is shown on the coordinate plane below.

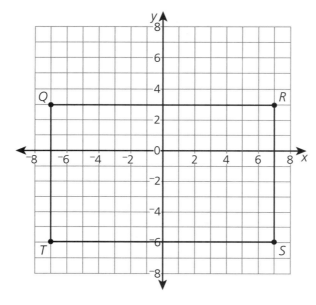

Part A What is the area, in square units, of rectangle *QRST*?

Answer _____

Part B Explain how you found your answer.

_____

_____

_____

UNIT 9
Data and Statistics

● **Lesson 1 Collecting Data** reviews what data are and what types of questions are used to collect data.

● **Lesson 2 Data Distributions** reviews what data distributions are and what measures of center and measures of spread are.

● **Lesson 3 Measures of Central Tendency** reviews what the mean, median, and mode of a data set are.

● **Lesson 4 Measures of Spread** reviews what the range, interquartile range, and mean absolute deviation of a data set are.

● **Lesson 5 Representing Data** reviews how to display data in dot plots, histograms, and box plots.

Collecting Data

6.SP.1

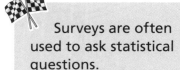

Surveys are often used to ask statistical questions.

A **statistical question** is a question that has different possible responses. **Data** is the information received as responses to statistical questions.

Which of these questions is a statistical question?

- What time is the next train expected?
- How often do students rent movies from the local video store?

The first question asks a specific question about time. Only one possible answer exists. So, this is not a statistical question.

The second question is aimed towards more than one person. A variety of data can be collected to answer this question since it is likely that different answers will result. So, this is a statistical question.

Statistical questions that are **quantitative** have numerical data. Statistical questions that are **qualitative** have non-numerical data.

What type of data, quantitative or qualitative, results from the statistical questions below?

- What is the most popular book among sixth graders?
- How old are the students in the dance class?

Numerical data are numbers, such as ages, counts of objects, or distances.

Non-numerical data are not numbers. They can be titles, colors, or opinions.

Data collected from the question about the most popular book will be titles of various books. Since these data are non-numerical, qualitative data results.

Data collected from the question about ages of the students will be numbers. These data are numerical, so quantitative data results.

SAMPLE Which of the following questions is *not* a statistical question?

   A Who is the manager of this store?

   B What is the favorite breakfast cereal in my school?

   C Where do teenagers shop for clothes?

   D How old were my classmates when they lost their first tooth?

The correct answer is A. A statistical question is one that has many possible answers. The question in choice A is not statistical because there is likely only one person who is the manager of a specific store. The questions in choices B, C, and D are statistical questions since there are different breakfast cereals, different places to shop for clothes, and different ages when people may have lost their first tooth.

1 Dawn conducts a survey about the shopping habits of teenagers. Which of the following best represents a quantitative response?

   A size medium

   B 50 East Street

   C one hundred dollars

   D every first Saturday

2 The owner of a restaurant asks customers to rank the service of the waitstaff on a scale from one to five. What type of data does this represent?

   A Qualitative because it is numerical.

   B Quantitative because it is numerical.

   C Qualitative because it is non-numerical.

   D Quantitative because it is non-numerical.

3 Which is a statistical question?

   A What is the price of a new watch?

   B How much does this watch cost?

   C What time does the baseball game start today?

   D How long is the movie you are watching?

4 Gabe asks his classmates, "What is our school mascot?" What type of question is this?

   A a statistical question with a qualitative response

   B a statistical question with a quantitative response

   C a non-statistical question with a qualitative response

   D a non-statistical question with a quantitative response

SAMPLE Nicholas asks his classmates to list all the books that they read during the last month. The data he collects from this question are qualitative. Explain how Nicholas can change this question to collect data that are quantitative.

_____

_____

✓ Qualitative data is non-numerical. Quantitative data is numerical. To rewrite this question to collect numerical data, Nicholas can ask his classmates how many books they read during the last month.

5 Write a possible survey question that represents a statistical question.

Answer _____

6 A survey asks responders how many hours a week they work. Would the data collected for this question be qualitative or quantitative?

Answer _____

7 Eva asks her teacher what the tallest building in the United States is. She thinks this represents a statistical question. Is Eva's thinking correct? Explain how you know.

_____

_____

8 Bryan writes two survey questions to ask his classmates. One question is quantitative. The other is qualitative.

> What makes a question qualitative? What makes a question quantitative?

Part A What are two possible questions that Bryan could ask?

Answer 1 _____

_____

Answer 2 _____

_____

Part B Explain why you chose the two questions you wrote in part A.

_____

_____

_____

9 Tanya asks the following question in a survey.

"Which pizzeria makes the best pizza?"

Part A From the list below, write all the words that describe this type of question.

statistical   non-statistical   qualitative   quantitative

Answer _____

Part B Explain how you know your answer is correct.

_____

_____

_____

Data Distributions

6.SP.2, 6.SP.3

The measure of center represents the typical value of a data set.

Center can also indicate accuracy. A high center has greater accuracy than a low center.

Low Center   High Center

The measure of spread compares the low value and the high value in a data set.

Spread can also indicate precision. A low spread has greater precision than a high spread.

Low Spread   High Spread

Skewed data has the majority of values to the left or right of the center.

Symmetric data is more evenly spread about the center.

A **data distribution** gives information about a data set using numbers. The number that represents the **center** summarizes all the numbers in the data set. This is called the **measure of center.** The number that represents the **spread** describes how the numbers in a data set vary. This is called the **measure of spread.**

Compare the two data sets below. Which data set has a greater spread?

Set A: {8, 9, 13, 16, 17, 19, 23, 39, 41, 46}
Set B: {61, 63, 64, 65, 68, 69, 70, 70, 72}

Look at how the numbers vary in each data set.

In set A, the smallest number is 8 and the largest number is 46. These numbers vary by about 40.

In set B, the smallest number is 61 and the largest number is 72. These numbers vary by about 10.

Even though the numbers in set B are greater than those in set A, the spread of set A is greater than that of set B.

The distribution of numbers in a data set has an overall shape. The shape can be described as **skewed to the left, skewed to the right,** or **symmetric.**

Describe the overall shape of set A above.

Of the 10 numbers in set A, 7 of them are less than 25 and 3 of them are greater than 25. Most of the numbers in this set have a smaller value. They are skewed to the left.

SAMPLE Which of the following sets of data can be described as being skewed to the right?

A {1, 6, 9, 13, 15, 20, 25, 28}   C {12, 14, 15, 19, 20, 29, 37}

B {24, 26, 28, 30, 32, 34, 36}   D {10, 13, 27, 29, 29, 31, 32}

The correct answer is D. A data set that is skewed to the right has the majority of numbers closer to the higher numbers in the set. The numbers in choices A and B do not appear centered about the low values or the high values. They are more symmetrical. The numbers in choice C appear centered more around the lower values, so this set is skewed to the left. The numbers in choice D, however, appear centered more around the higher values, so this set is skewed to the right.

1 The grades each student received on a history report are listed below in order from least to greatest.

```
65  70  72  72  79
80  80  84  88  90
91  93  95  95  97
```

Which number best represents the center of the data?

A   32   C   84

B   65   D   97

2 Which plot shows data that is skewed to the left?

3 Hal wrote the number 150 to describe the data in this list: 98, 111, 129, 150, 157, 164, 168, 169, 175, 178, 182, 195, 199, 247. Which statement best describes this number?

A   It is a measure of center since it represents a typical data value.

B   It is a measure of spread since it represents a typical data value.

C   It is a measure of center since it shows how much the data vary.

D   It is a measure of spread since it shows how much the data vary.

4 The ages of people who answered a survey at the local park are as follows: 21, 24, 26, 27, 27, 33, 39, 45, 52, 62. Which number is closest to the spread of the data?

A   20   C   40

B   30   D   60

SAMPLE The plots below show the grades each student in a math class received on two quizzes.

QUIZ 1 GRADES					
5					
6	5				
7	0	0	5		
8	0	0	0	5	5
9	0	5	5	5	
10	0				

7|5 means 75

QUIZ 2 GRADES					
5					
6					
7	5	5	5	5	
8	5	5	5	5	5	5
9	0	0	0	5	
10					

7|5 means 75

On which quiz, 1 or 2, do the grades have the lower spread? Explain how you know.

_____

_____

> The data with the lower spread has grades that are closer together. On quiz 1, the grades range from 65 to 100. On quiz 2, the range in grades is smaller, from 75 to 95. So the grades on quiz 2 have a lower spread.

5 A data set containing six numbers has a spread of 50. What could be the numbers in the data set?

Answer _____

6 The numbers below represent the bowling scores of nine different bowlers.

127   129   129   130   131   133   140   169   205

Is 133 a reasonable number to represent the measure of center for these bowling scores? Explain how you know.

_____

_____

7 A company has workers on a day shift and a night shift. The line plots below show the number of hours the workers on each shift typically work each day.

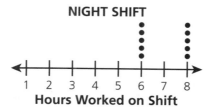

Part A Which data set has a greater measure of center—the day shift or the night shift? Explain how you know.

> What number of hours are the data points from each data set closest to?

_____

_____

_____

Part B Which data set has a greater measure of spread—the day shift or the night shift? Explain how you know.

_____

_____

_____

Measures of central tendency represent the typical value of a data set. The larger the data set, the more representative the measure.

The mean is sometimes call the average.

Measures of center are sometimes called **measures of central tendency.** They include the mean, the median, and the mode.

The **mean** is the average of all the values. To find the mean, sum all the numbers in the data set. Then divide the sum by the number of values in the data set.

> This list shows the length, in minutes, of the first ten phone calls received at a customer service center one day.
>
> 6   15   13   3   4   5   3   2   1   8
>
> What is the mean length of the phone calls?
>
> Find the sum of all the values.
>
> $$6 + 15 + 13 + 3 + 4 + 5 + 3 + 2 + 1 + 8 = 60$$
>
> Divide the sum by 10, the number of data values in the set.
>
> $$60 \div 10 = 6$$
>
> The mean length of the calls is 6 minutes.

Data can be ordered from low to high or from high to low when finding the median. The same median will result.

If there is an even number of data points, the median is the average of the two middle values.

The **median** is the middle value in an ordered data set.

> What is the median length of the phone calls?
>
> First, order the data values. Then find the middle value.
>
> 1   2   3   3   4   5   6   8   13   15
>
> There are two middle values, 4 and 5. The average of these numbers is 4.5. The median length is 4.5 minutes.

A data set can have no mode, exactly one mode, or more than one mode.

The **mode** is the number that appears most often in a data set.

> What is the mode length of the phone calls?
>
> Look for the values that appear most often. The number 3 is the only value that is repeated in the data set. So, the mode is 3 minutes.

SAMPLE The age of each employee at a mall store is listed below.

19 21 21 23 23 23 25 28 32 33 36 64

Which of the following measures of central tendency would be best for summarizing the data?

A mean only

B mode only

C mean or median

D mode or median

The correct answer is D. The mean of the data is 29. The median of the data is 24 and the mode is 23. The mean is higher than most of the data values because of the high value 64. So this is not a good measure. The median and the mode are close in value and better measures of the data.

1 Harry wants to survey students at his school about what time they arrive at school on a typical morning. Which group is most likely to give him accurate measures for his data?

A 10 students on his bus

B 25 students in the lunchroom

C 75 students in different homerooms

D 100 students practicing sports before school

2 A survey asks people to name their favorite type of car. Which measure of central tendency is best to use for summarizing the typical response to this survey?

A mean only

B mode only

C mean and median

D mode and median

3 The baking times, in minutes, for different casserole recipes are listed here: 30, 45, 60, 45, 90, 60, 55, 75, 40, 45. What is the median baking time?

A 30 minutes

B 45 minutes

C 50 minutes

D 75 minutes

4 The prices of houses sold on one street are listed below.

$145,000	$150,000	$165,000
$139,000	$142,000	$361,000
$154,000	$148,000	$162,000

Which statement best explains why the mean would not be a good measure of central tendency for the data?

A There are only nine pieces of data.

B No two prices are the same.

C The prices are too large to measure.

D One price is significantly higher than all the others.

SAMPLE The data below shows the number of minutes each person stretched before a fitness class.

10	5	5	10	10	5	10	10
10	10	10	5	45	15	10	45

Which measure of central tendency—mean, median, or mode—would best represent the data? Explain how you know.

_____

_____

> Either the median or the mode would be best since they are both 10. The mean is likely to be higher than most of the times in the data set because of the two values of 45 that are significantly higher than the other data points. So it would not be a good measure.

5 A data set contains eight numbers and has a median of 50. What could be the numbers in the data set?

Answer _____

6 Carol had 19 shoppers fill out a survey on Saturday and 51 shoppers fill out a survey on Sunday. Which day are the results of the survey more likely to be representative of all shoppers, Saturday or Sunday? Explain how you know.

_____

_____

7 Describe a situation where the mode would not be a good measure of central tendency.

_____

_____

8 This table shows the number of points scored by each player on a sports team during a game.

POINTS SCORED BY TEAM

Points	0	1	2	3	4	5
Number of Players	1	3	1	2	0	1

Part A How many data values are in this data set?

Answer _____

Part B Explain how you know.

_____

_____

9 The list below shows the numbers of words contestants in a spelling bee spelled correctly.

6 9 5 10 4 1 2 1 9 3

Part A What is the mean number of words spelled correctly?

Answer _____

Part B Explain why the mode would **not** be a good measure of central tendency for the data above.

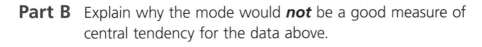 How do you find the mode of a data set? It may help to write the data values in order before finding the mode.

_____

_____

_____

Measures of Spread

6.SP.5.a–d

Measures of spread show **variation,** or how far values within a data set differ from each other.

Measures of spread describe how the numbers in a data set vary. They include the range, the interquartile range, and the mean absolute deviation.

The **range** is the difference between the highest and lowest values in a data set.

> This list shows the distances Craig rode his bike, in miles, each day last week: 8, 3, 7, 14, 18, 11, 2.
>
> What is the range of these distances?
>
> Order the data: 2   3   7   8   11   14   18
>
> Find the difference between the highest and lowest values.
>
> $$18 - 2 = 16$$
>
> The range is 16 miles.

The **interquartile range** is the range of the middle 50% of an ordered data set.

> What is the interquartile range for distances above?
>
> First, find the middle value of the data:
>
>   2   3   7   ⑧   11   14   18
>
> Next, find the middle values of the data to the left and right of 8.
>
>   2   ③   7   ⑧   11   ⑭   18
>
> Finally, find the difference between these two middle values.
>
> $$14 - 3 = 11$$
>
> The interquartile range is 11 miles.

The **mean absolute deviation** is the number that shows the average difference between the mean and each value in a data set. If the mean absolute deviation is small, the values in the data set are close to the mean. If it is large, the values are far away from the mean.

If the number of data points is even, the median, or middle of a data set, is the average of the two middle values.

To find the mean of a data set, first sum all the data values. Then divide the sum by the number of data values in the set.

mean of bike distances =

$$\frac{2 + 3 + 7 + 8 + 11 + 14 + 18}{7} =$$

$$\frac{63}{7} = 9$$

SAMPLE Which data set has the smallest mean absolute deviation?

A {1, 2, 3, 4, 5}   **C** {100, 100, 100, 100, 100}

B {10, 20, 30, 40, 50}   **D** (1,000, 1,100, 1,110, 1,111}

The correct answer is C. The mean of these data is 100. Since all the values in the data set equal the mean, the difference between the mean and each value is 0. The data sets in choices A, B, and D will all have differences greater than 0 for the mean absolute deviation. So choice C is has the smallest value.

1 The cost of each calculator at a store is listed below.

| $24 | $89 | $9 | $5 |
| $99 | $99 | $133 | $119 |

What is the range in these prices?

A $95   **C** $128

B $124   **D** $133

2 Shauna wants to find the mean absolute deviation of the data below.

NUMBER OF PETS IN HOME

Number of Pets	0	1	2	3	4 or more
Number of Homes	8	14	3	2	7

What is the total number of data values in this data set?

A 4   **C** 26

B 10   **D** 34

3 The wait times, in minutes, for clients at an office one morning are listed below.

3   6   10   12   15   15   18   20   20

What is the interquartile range of the data?

A 8   **C** 15

B 11   **D** 17

4 The data sets on the following number lines each have a mean of 6. Which number line has data with the greatest absolute deviation from the mean?

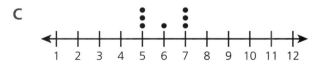

SAMPLE The data below show the years of experience that each math teacher at Logan Middle School has.

5   13   18   26   4   10   31   9   15

Which measure of spread—range, interquartile range, or mean absolute deviation—would **not** be the best representation of the variation in the data? Explain.

_____

_____

The range is limited in the variability it shows since only the high and low values in the data set are used. Nothing about the other data values is known. So the range is not the best measure. With the interquartile range, more information is known about the data values since the middle 50% of the data is being analyzed. The mean absolute deviation tells more about the data than the other two measures. For any data set, you can tell how close the data values are to the mean based on the size of the mean absolute deviation.

5 A data set contains seven numbers and has a range of 50. What could be the numbers in the data set?

Answer _____

6 What is the interquartile range of the data below?

75   125   25   15   50   120   105

Answer _____

7 The base prices for the top-selling laptop computers in a catalog are listed below.

$499 $299 $449 $379 $999 $799 $749 $599

Part A What is the range of the data?

Answer _____

Part B Explain why the mean absolute deviation is a better measure of spread for the data than the range.

_____

_____

_____

_____

8 Set X and set Y each have 5 data values. The mean absolute deviation of set X is much greater than the mean absolute deviation of set Y.

Part A Write possible data values for both set X and set Y.

Set X _____

Set Y _____

What does a large mean absolute deviation tell you about how close the values in a data set are?

Part B Explain why you chose the data values you did for both sets.

_____

_____

_____

Representing Data

6.SP.4

Dot plots are good for showing countable data whose values are close together.

Each dot on the plot represents a year in the table. Since the table shows ten years, there are ten dots on the plot.

In a histogram, the intervals are equal in size and contain no gaps and no overlaps.

The five key points of a box-and-whisker plot are placed along a number line and connected with "boxes" in the middle and "whiskers" at each end.

Data displays organize and make data easy to read. Dot plots, histograms, and box plots are three types of data displays. A **dot plot** is a display that stacks dots above a number line to show the shape of data. It is also called a line plot and may use X's instead of dots.

This table shows the number of foreign exchange students that visited Hillary's school during the past ten years.

FOREIGN EXCHANGE STUDENTS

Year	1	2	3	4	5	6	7	8	9	10
Number of Students	6	3	5	6	0	3	8	6	6	8

Draw a dot plot to show the data in the table.

Draw a number line. The scale refers to the number of students. Draw a dot above the correct number of students for each year.

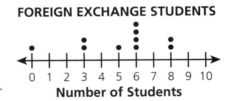

FOREIGN EXCHANGE STUDENTS

Number of Students

A **histogram** is like a bar graph that shows data in intervals. There are no spaces between the bars.

Draw a histogram to show the data in the table and dot plot above.

Choose an appropriate interval for the range of each bar, the number of students. Then find the number of years that fall into each range. Draw bars up to that number.

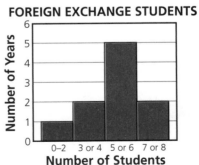

FOREIGN EXCHANGE STUDENTS

Number of Years

Number of Students

A **box plot,** also called a **box-and-whisker plot,** is a graph that summarizes five key data points from a data set: the minimum, the maximum, the median, and the points from the interquartile range.

SAMPLE Roger made a box plot to summarize the data below.

124   118   129   139   133   129   142   135   122   137

What are the five key data points on the box plot?

A 118, 124, 131, 137, 142   **C** 124, 129, 131, 135, 137

B 118, 129, 133, 135, 142   **D** 124, 129, 133, 135, 142

The correct answer is A. First list the data in order: 118, 122, 124, 129, 129, 133, 135, 137, 139, 142. The minimum is 118. The maximum is 142. The median is 131, the average of the two middle numbers 129 and 133. The middle number to the left of the median is 124. The middle number to the right of the median is 137. The five key data points are 118, 124, 131, 137, and 142.

1 The hourly rates of ten employees at a company are listed below.

$12	$18	$10	$9	$11
$16	$15	$12	$12	$10

What is the most appropriate range along the number line for a dot plot of the data?

A 0–10   **C** 8–20

B 0–30   **D** 8–40

2 This histogram shows the ages, in years, of the houses in a neighborhood.

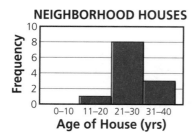

How many houses are 21–30 years old?

A 6   **C** 8

B 7   **D** 10

3 The scores from the Tigers' first nine baseball games are listed below.

4   1   7   3   5   3   4   7   1

Which box plot summarizes the data?

A
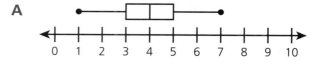

B
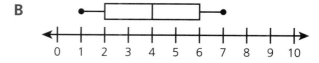

C
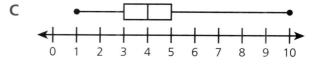

D
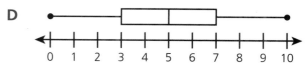

SAMPLE The data below shows the ages, in years, of each pet adopted from an animal shelter last week.

| 2 | 4 | 1 | 6 | 9 | 2 | 1 | 11 | 6 | 4 |
| 1 | 1 | 4 | 7 | 2 | 3 | 5 | 8 | 2 | 3 |

Draw a dot plot to show the data. Be sure to give the dot plot a title and label it appropriately.

Choose a range for the number line of the dot plot. The smallest data value is 1. The largest is 11. So an appropriate range would be from 0 to 12. Draw a number line with this range. Place a dot over each number on the number line to represent each data point. There are 20 data values in all, so there should be 20 dots on the plot. Give the graph a title and a label for the number line to describe what it shows.

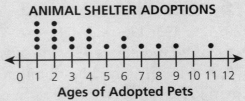

4 The number of people in each tour group at an historical attraction one day is listed below.

| 20 | 13 | 15 | 22 | 16 | 28 | 20 | 12 |

Draw a box plot to summarize the data. Be sure to give the box plot a title and label each of the key points on the plot.

5 The number of hours each employee at a bakery is scheduled to work next week is listed below.

| 30 | 24 | 32 | 40 | 16 | 8 | 40 |
| 28 | 24 | 30 | 20 | 24 | 20 | 32 |

The owner of the bakery will make a histogram to display the number of hours of the employees.

Part A What is an appropriate interval for each bar in the histogram?

What are the minimum and maximum data values? Be sure to find an interval that includes both of these and that isn't too big or too small.

Answer _____

Part B Draw a histogram to show the data. Be sure to label each axis appropriately and give the histogram a title.

REVIEW

Data and Statistics

Read each problem. Circle the letter of the best answer.

1 The number of hours each volunteer at a community center worked one day is listed here: 6, 4, 5, 2, 6, 4, 2, 3, 8, 3. Which statement is true of the data?

A The mean is 5. **C** The mode is 6.

B The range is 3. **D** The median is 4.

2 The number of long distance phone calls Lisa made each month is listed below.

8	0	16	3	20	29
0	11	20	9	12	18

Which statement best explains why the mode would not be a good measure of central tendency for the data?

A 0 cannot be a mode.

B There is an outlier in the data.

C There are only twelve pieces of data.

D There are two modes far apart in value.

3 The number of children in each classroom of a preschool are listed here: 7, 8, 8, 10, 12, 13, 15, 15. What is the interquartile range of the data?

A 6 **C** 9

B 8 **D** 11

4 Which type of question is below?

"How many vacations did company employees take last year?"

A a statistical question with a qualitative response

B a statistical question with a quantitative response

C a non-statistical question with a qualitative response

D a non-statistical question with a quantitative response

5 The age of each singer in a chorus is listed below.

19	16	17	15	19	15
15	19	19	20	17	20

Which dot plot shows the data?

A

C

B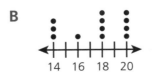

D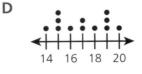

6 Write a possible survey question that represents a statistical question.

Answer _____

7 The mean of the data below is 7.

Will the mean absolute deviation of the data be a small number or a large number? Explain how you know.

_____

_____

8 Scott's first ten homework grades are listed below.

60   70   70   75   75   80   85   85   85   85

Is 80 a reasonable number to represent the measure of center for these homework grades? Explain how you know.

_____

_____

9 A histogram will be made of the data below.

170   178   189   215   233   262   267   288   304
312   316   321   345   360   360   376   380   385

Describe an appropriate interval for each bar in the histogram.

Answer _____

10 This table shows the points Valerie scored on a dartboard.

POINTS SCORED ON DARTBOARD

Points	0	10	25	50	100
Number of Throws	1	1	9	13	6

Part A How many data values are in this data set?

Answer _____

Part B Explain how you know.

_____

_____

11 The number of sales Luis made each month last year is listed below.

5	9	15	11	9	13
16	23	35	22	15	12

Part A What is the median of the data?

Answer _____

Part B Draw a box plot to show the data. Be sure to give the box plot a title and label each of the key points on the plot.

PRACTICE TEST

Read each problem. Circle the letter of the best answer.

1 Which situation can best be described using a negative integer?

   A   2 dollars an hour raise

   B   50 feet below sea level

   C   30 minutes ahead of time

   D   10 percent interest earned

2 Five cars are parked in a lot. What is the ratio of tires to steering wheels for these cars?

   A   5 to 1   **C**   10 to 5

   B   10 to 4   **D**   20 to 5

3 A cashier serviced 72 customers in 3 hours. What unit rate describes the number of customers serviced each hour?

   A   3 customers per hour

   B   24 customers per hour

   C   32 customers per hour

   D   72 customers per hour

4 Isabel earned $8,400 in a 24-week period. She earned the same amount of money each week. What amount of money did she earn each of those weeks?

   A $200   **C** $350

   B $240   **D** $400

5 Which of the following questions best represents a statistical question?

   A   Where is the local mall?

   B   What time does this store open?

   C   Who is the owner of that restaurant?

   D   How many hours a week do waiters work?

6 A pumpkin weighs 29.3125 pounds. A squash weighs 3.75 pounds. How much greater is the weight of the pumpkin than the weight of the squash?

   A   8.1875 pounds

   B   25.5625 pounds

   C   26.4375 pounds

   D   33.0625 pounds

7 Which number line shows the opposite of the opposite of –3?

A

B

C

D

8 Cassandra read 25 pages of a 125-page book. What percent of the book did she read?

A 15%   **C** 25%

B 20%   **D** 40%

9 Ronald wants to solve the equation $m + 7 = 23$. What should he do to both sides of the equation?

A add 7   **C** add 23

B subtract 7   **D** subtract 23

10 Use this number line to help answer the question.

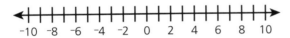

Which statement is true?

A $-|2| = -2$ **C** $|-6| = -6$

B $-|-4| = 4$ **D** $-|8| = 8$

11 What two terms are being multiplied in the expression $5(x + 8)$?

A 5 and x **C** 5 and $8x$

B 8 and x **D** 5 and $x + 8$

12 There are 36 girls and 40 boys at a summer camp. The campers will be divided into equal-sized groups. Each group will have the same number of girls and the same number of boys. What is the greatest number of groups that can be formed?

A 4   **C** 8

B 6   **D** 12

13 What is the missing value in the table below?

n	$n^2 + 4$
1	5
2	8
3	13
4	?

A 16   **C** 20

B 18   **D** 22

14 Meg has 6 charm bracelets. Each bracelet has 12 charms on it. Which expression can be used to find the number of charms on all of Meg's bracelets?

A $6 + 12$ **C** 6×12

B $12 - 6$ **D** $12 \div 6$

15 Which inequality statement is true?

A $-1 < -2$ **C** $4 < -6$

B $-3 < 0$ **D** $-8 < -10$

16 Use this number line to help answer the question.

Which inequality statement is true?

A $-6 < -2 < 1$ **C** $-2 < -6 < 1$

B $-6 > -2 > 1$ **D** $-2 > -6 > 1$

17 Which number sentence is true?

A $x + (y - z) = xy - xz$

B $x + (y \times z) = (x + y) \times z$

C $(x + y) + z = z + (x + y)$

D $x - (y - z) = (x - y) - z$

18 The quotient of 6 and n is 3. Which equation models this?

A $\dfrac{6}{n} = 3$

C $6 \times n = 3$

B $\dfrac{n}{6} = 3$

D $6 - n = 3$

19 A cheetah can run 3,300 feet in 30 seconds. Which fraction shows how fast the cheetah can run, in feet per second, written in lowest terms?

A $\dfrac{100}{1}$

C $\dfrac{100}{3}$

B $\dfrac{110}{1}$

D $\dfrac{110}{3}$

20 A bottle contains 240 milliliters of juice. How many liters of juice is this?

A 0.0240

C 24,000

B 0.240

D 240,000

21 Which value of r makes the scale below balanced?

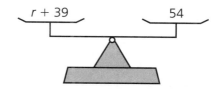

A 15

C 83

B 25

D 93

22 Which expression is equivalent to $c + 2$?

A $c + 2c$

C $3c - 3 + c + 1$

B $2c - 2c + 2$

D $4c + 6 - 3c - 4$

23 A trapezoid has base lengths of 5 cm and 9 cm and a height of 6 cm. What is the area of the trapezoid?

A 42 cm^2

C 135 cm^2

B 84 cm^2

D 270 cm^2

24 The number of points Jake has in a video game is 2 times as great as the number of points Marc has. Jake has at most 12 points. Which number line shows the possible points Marc has?

A

B
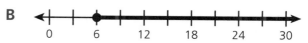

C
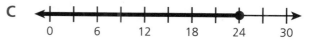

D

25 Which graph shows the function $y = 3x$?

A

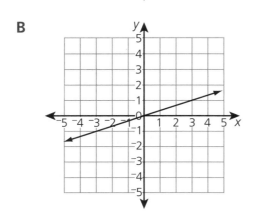

B

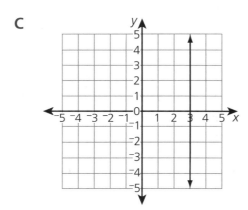

C

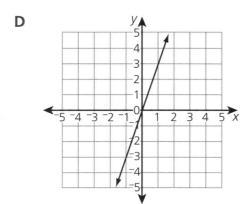

D

26 The formula for the approximate surface area of a sphere with a radius of r centimeters is shown below.

$$SA = 4(3)(r^2)$$

What is the approximate surface area, in square centimeters, of a sphere with a radius of 20 centimeters?

A 480 cm^2 **C** 4,800 cm^2

B 720 cm^2 **D** 7,200 cm^2

27 What is the rule for this input-output table?

Input	Output
4	12
6	14
8	16
10	18

A add 2   **C** multiply by 2

B add 8   **D** multiply by 3

28 A mailbox is represented by the diagram below.

4 ft

$2\frac{1}{2}$ ft

$2\frac{1}{2}$ ft

What is the volume of the mailbox?

A 9 ft^2 **C** 25 ft^3

B 10 ft^2 **D** 40 ft^3

29 The number of vacation days each employee at a small company has is listed below.

    11 5 5 10 8 12 7 10 10

Which statement is true of the data?

A The mean is 10.   **C** The range is 7.

B The mode is 5.   **D** The median is 8.

30 The value of d in the inequality below represents the depth, in feet, of a cave.

$$d < \text{-}16$$

Which statement best describes d?

A The depth of the cave is 16 feet below ground.

B The depth of the cave is 16 feet above ground.

C The depth of the cave is less than 16 feet below ground.

D The depth of the cave is greater than 16 feet below ground.

31 A store received a shipment of 160 T-shirts. Of these, 30 were small, 60 were medium, and the rest were large. What is the ratio of large T-shirts to small T-shirts? Write your answer three different ways.

Answer _____

32 The opposite of the opposite of a number is 7. What is the number?

Answer _____

33 A function machine is shown below.

Input	Output
4 →	→ 8
16 →	→ 20

What is the output from this function machine when the input is 50?

Answer _____

34 Cara and Jane multiplied the numbers 2.005 and 0.3. Cara got an answer of 6.015. Jane got an answer of 0.6015. Who got the correct answer, Cara or Jane? Explain how you know.

_____

_____

_____

35 What is the missing number in this table?

7	11	14	20
21	33	?	60

Answer _____

36 A package contains 3 cups of trail mix. A serving of trail mix is $\frac{1}{3}$ cup. How many servings of trail mix are in the package?

Answer _____

37 A 6-month membership costs $180. At this rate, how much would a 9-month membership cost?

Answer _____

38 Draw and label the polygon with vertices L (−3, 6), M (6, 3), N (6, −6), and P (−3, 0) on the coordinate plane below.

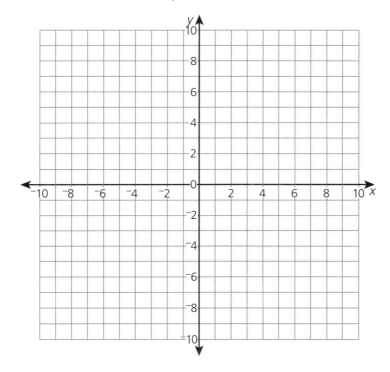

39 What conversion factors are used to convert gallons per hour to quarts per minute?

Answer _____

40 Connor found that 60% of 40 is the same as 25% of another number, *n.* What is the value of *n?*

Answer _____

41 Paper plates come in packages of 60. Napkins come in packages of 80. Natasha wants the same number of plates and napkins for a school dance. What is the fewest number of plates she will need to get?

Answer _____

42 The net for a storage trunk is represented below.

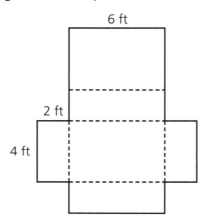

What is the surface area, in square feet, of the trunk?

Answer _____

43 Name a point that is located in quadrant III on a coordinate plane.

Answer _____

44 What is the value of the expression $8 + (7 - 3)^2 \div 4 \times 2$?

Answer _____

45 Glen made this shape using rectangles and triangles.

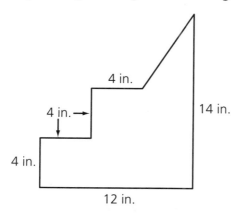

4 in.

4 in. →

14 in.

4 in.

12 in.

What is the area, in square inches, of the shape?

Answer _____

46 The costs, in dollars, of the top-selling digital cameras at a store are listed below.

336   159   144   200   700   70   159   289   419   280

What is a reasonable number to represent the measure of center?

Answer _____

47 Jayden wants to solve the equation $n + 67 = 81$. He writes the equation $n + 67 - 67 = 81 - 67$ to find the value of n. Will Jayden get the correct answer using this equation? Explain how you know.

_____

_____

48 Are the expressions $5(2d + 6)$ and $10d + 6$ equivalent? Explain how you know.

_____

_____

49 Of the numbers 8, 9, 10, 11, and 12, which are solutions to the inequality $8p < 84$?

Answer _____

50 The times, in minutes, it took 16 students to complete a logic puzzle are listed below.

| 15 | 11 | 9 | 15 | 12 | 10 | 18 | 16 |
| 14 | 22 | 13 | 20 | 17 | 12 | 18 | 19 |

Draw a box plot to show the data. Be sure to give the box plot a title and label each of the key points on the plot.

51 Grape juice comes in a 64-ounce bottle. Apple juice comes in an 80-ounce bottle. Both juices will be poured into cups of equal size so that no juice remains in either bottle.

Part A Can each type of juice be poured into 4-ounce cups? Explain how you know.

_____

_____

Part B How many ounces is the largest cup possible that can be used for the juices?

Answer _____

52 Rectangle QRST is shown on the coordinate plane below.

Part A What quadrant is the rectangle located in?

Answer _____

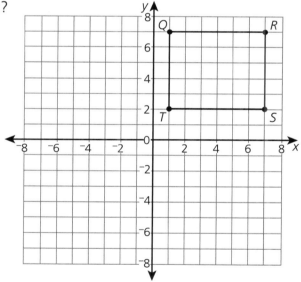

Part B What is the length, in units, of side QR? Explain how you know.

_____

_____

_____

53 Tabitha wrote the function $y = x + 3$.

Part A Make an x–y table of values to model this function for
x-values 0, 2, 4, and 6.

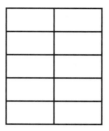

Part B Graph this function on the coordinate plane below. Be sure
to label each axis with appropriate values.

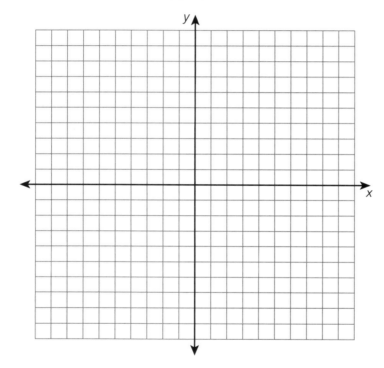

GLOSSARY

absolute value — the distance of a number from 0 on a number line

algebraic expression — an expression that contains symbols, or letters, and numbers and operations

align — to line up

area — the space inside a plane figure, measured in square units

area formulas — equations used to find the area of plane figures:

rectangle: $A = lw = \text{length} \times \text{width}$

parallelogram: $A = bh = \text{base} \times \text{height}$

triangle: $A = \frac{1}{2}bh = \frac{1}{2} \times \text{base} \times \text{height}$

trapezoid: $A = \frac{1}{2}(b_1 + b_2)h = \frac{1}{2} \times (\text{base}_1 + \text{base}_2) \times \text{height}$

associative property — allows grouping of numbers with parentheses to be added or multiplied: $a + (b + c) = (a + b) + c$ and $a \times (b \times c) = (a \times b) \times c$

box plot — a data display that identifies five key measures of a data set: the minimum, the maximum, the median, and the points from the interquartile range

box-and-whisker plot — a box plot

common factor — a factor that two or more whole numbers share

common multiple — a multiple that two or more whole numbers share

commutative property — allows numbers to be added or multiplied in any order: $a + b = b + a$ and $a \times b = b \times a$

conversion factor — a ratio of equal measure used to change a rate with one set of measurements to another

convert — to change

coordinate plane	the space defined by two number lines placed at right angles and used to locate points in space in relation to their distances from the number lines
cubic units	units that are cubed, or raised to the 3rd power

D — **data** — information received as responses to statistical questions

data displays	ways to organize and make data easy to read, such as graphs and plots
data distribution	a description of a data set
decimal quotient	a quotient that continues to the right of the decimal point, representing the remainder in whole number division
denominator	the bottom number of a fraction; it tells how many parts in the whole or set
dependent variable	the *y*-variable, or the output
distributive property	allows a number to be multiplied by a sum or each addend to be multiplied separately and the products added: $a(b + c) = ab + ac$
dividend	the number being divided in a division problem
divisor	the number that does the dividing in a division problem
dot plot	a display that stacks dots above a number line to show the shape of data; a line plot

E — **equation** — a mathematical statement that shows two expressions are equal

equivalent expressions	expressions that represent the same value
equivalent ratios	two or more ratios that compare the same quantities
evaluate	to find the value of a numerical or algebraic expression
expression	a grouping of numbers, symbols, and operations that show the value of something

F factors — whole numbers that multiply to form a product

function — a relationship between values of one set of numbers to another set

G greatest common factor — the largest of the common factors between two or more numbers

H histogram — a display that represents data in continuous intervals with adjacent bars

I independent variable — the *x*-variable, or the input

inequality — a mathematical statement that compares two expressions using inequality symbols

inequality symbols — relationship symbols used to make comparisons:

is less than ($<$)

is greater than ($>$)

is less than or equal to ($\leq$)

is greater than or equal to ($\geq$)

infinite — countless

input — first set of numbers in a function, the independent or *x*-variable

input-output table — function table

integer — a whole number that can be positive, negative, or zero

interquartile range — the range of the middle 50% of an ordered data set

inverse operations — opposite operations. Addition and subtraction are inverse operations. Multiplication and division are inverse operations.

L least common multiple — the smallest of the common multiples between two or more numbers

linear function — a function represented by a straight line

lowest terms — a ratio or fraction in which the terms cannot be divided by a number other than 1

 **mean** — the sum of the data values divided by the number of values; the average

mean absolute deviation — the number that shows the average difference between the mean and each value in a data set

measure of center — a number that summarizes all the numbers in the data set, including mean, median, and mode

measures of central tendency — measures of center

measure of spread — a number that describes how the numbers in a data set vary

median — the number in the middle of a set of data values

mixed number — a whole number plus a fraction

mode — the most common value in a data set

multiple — the product of a number and a nonzero whole number

 negative integer — an integer less than 0

net — a two-dimensional representation of a three-dimensional object

numerator — the top number of a fraction; it tells how many parts are talked about

numerical expression — an expression containing only numbers and operations

 opposites — numbers that are the same distance from 0

order of operations — the order in which operations are performed in a multi-operation expression: parentheses, exponents, multiplication and division from left to right, addition and subtraction from left to right

ordered pair — two numbers that name the location of a point on a coordinate plane; (x, y)

origin — the center of a coordinate plane, located at the intersection of the x- and y-axes, having the coordinates $(0, 0)$

output — second set of numbers in a function, the dependent or y-variable

P

percent	a ratio that compares a number to 100, written with the symbol %
percent equation	an equation used to help solve percent problems: *whole × percent = part*
polygon	a plane geometric figure with straight sides
positive integer	an integer greater than 0

Q

quadrants	the four regions a coordinate plane is divided into
qualitative data	non-numerical data, such as colors and opinions
quantitative data	numerical data, such as measurements and counts
quantities	numbers or amounts
quotient	the answer to a division problem

R

range	the difference between the highest and lowest values in a data set
rate	a comparison between two quantities with different units of measure
ratio	a comparison of two numbers
rational numbers	numbers that can be expressed as ratios
reciprocal	the number by which another number is multiplied to equal a product of 1
rectangular prism	a solid figure with all rectangular faces

S

skewed to the left	having more data values at the low end
skewed to the right	having more data values at the high end
solution	the value of the variable that makes an equation true
solution set	all the values that make an inequality true
square units	units that are squared, or raised to the 2nd power
statistical question	a question to which responses vary
substitute	to replace
surface area	the sum of the areas of each side of an object
symmetric data	having evenly distributed data values

 **three-dimensional**   a solid figure with length, width, and height
figure

two-step equation   an equation requiring more than one operation to solve

unit cube   a cube with a side length of 1 unit and a volume of 1 cubic unit

unit rate   a rate that compares a quantity to one unit

variables   letters or symbols that represent values that can change

variation   how far values within a data set differ from each other

vertex   a corner of a plane or solid figure

volume   the amount of space inside a three-dimensional figure

x-axis   the horizontal axis of a coordinate plane

x-coordinate   the first number in an ordered pair, it names the horizontal position of a point

y-axis   the vertical axis of a coordinate plane

y-coordinate   the second number in an ordered pair, it names the vertical position of a point